MW01278116

Efficient Information Searching on the Web

A Handbook in the Art of Searching for Information

Jonas Fransson

Efficient Information Searching on the Web
A Handbook in the Art of Searching for Information

ISBN: 978-81-7000-637-4

Rs.575/-

First Published 2011

Published by:
Ess Ess Publications
4837/24, Ansari Road,
Darya Ganj,
New Delhi-110 002.
INDIA
Phones: 23260807, 41563444
Fax: 41563334
E-mail: info@essessreference.com
www.essessreference.com

Cover Design by *Patch Creative Unit*

Printed and bound in India at Salasar Imaging Systems.

Contents

Preface

To seek information is one of the most common occupations on the Web. We search for information in a number of different situations and for different purposes. We often make use of search services to try to find the information that we are looking for. But what is it really that we are looking for and how do we get there? Is it enough to just "google" or does it take more? How does it actually work? There are many myths about search services, particularly about search engines such as Google. I hope that this book will clear up some part of the mystical fog that surrounds the activity of searching on the Web and at the same time my hopes are that the book will encourage discussion and mutual learning.

This edition is an updated and adapted version of the first Swedish edition which came out in November 2007. Many of the examples have been substituted by others, but at times typically Swedish examples have been left as they stand. Hopefully the "Swedish" element will not interfere with the reading, but instead add a touch of Sweden and further a reading where the reader's own, more immediate examples can come into play.

I want to thank everyone who has read the Swedish edition. Especially, I want to thank Inger Pettersson who, meritoriously, has translated into English. Any errors that may occur in the book are mine alone, and nobody else's. I would gladly receive comments and suggestions for improvement via email at jonas@jonasfransson.com. Get in touch!

Welcome to a world of constant and exciting changes!

Jonas Fransson

Lund, Sweden, 2009

Introduction

Information searching on the Web is unbelievably multifaceted. Many different roads often lead to the same information. All of us can do it differently and still reach the goal. But sometimes there seems to be no road whatsoever leading to where you want to go. When this happens it might be good to know about a few navigation tools.

When searching the Web many factors come into play. A lot of know-how and skills are useful when searching. At first sight some of the topics of the book may seem irrelevant or unnecessary, but my personal experience is that everything has its given place. The different pieces form a whole. For example, knowledge of html (Web page description language) leads up to an increased understanding of the structure and limitations of a search engine.

When it comes to search engines in the book I often speak of Google in the first place, giving examples in Google, etc. In most cases the same (or similar) goes for the other search engines, but Google has de facto become the standard when it comes to search engines. Google is today the most used search engine and probably the one that has most Web pages in its index. But Google has a couple of great challengers (Yahoo! and Live Search) so next year Google is perhaps neither the largest one nor the most popular one.

Google is not only the most used search engine but also an advertisement service of great proportions. The company's great profits come from the sales of so-called sponsored links which are shown on search pages. Critics mean that Google has cast its eye too much in the direction of commercial advertising and trade and that other search engines are better for information seekers today.

Information searching on the Web is very forgiving. Very few things are entirely wrong and it is possible to get to the same place in different ways. Examples of modes of procedure are:

+ following your own bookmark in the Web browser
+ writing a known address into the Web browser
+ guessing the address and writing it into the Web browser
+ browsing a link collection (browsing = systematic surfing)
+ searching in a search engine
+ using a meta-search service

Being out on the Web can be very frustrating. You can't find the page you visited the other day, the search engine is not delivering anything of interest when you search or the form which you are trying to fill in doesn't even accept the information. Researchers have started talking about *web rage* or *search rage* to describe the reactions caused by the frustration that sets in. Things don't work out the way you want them to and you don't know why.

Still more often users on the Web settle for second-rate results obtained through the search, though much better or more relevant hits were within reach. Why? Many times the average user's knowledge is quite insufficient, especially when searching on a new topic. With bigger knowledge, and perhaps more patience and perseverance, everybody's searches can become more efficient.

1. The Basics

Internet and the Web

What really are the Internet, the Net and the Web? Strictly speaking the Internet refers to a worldwide network which for the most part consists of computers and fibre-optic cables. The Web (www or the World Wide Web) consists of Web pages which are read by a Web browser (e.g., the Internet Explorer). The Web builds on the physical network constituted by the Internet. The Internet is in reality a number of computers connected through network cables that communicate with each other through the use of a common language, i.e. a network and nothing else. Web sites (a number of connected Web pages) are on a so-called Web server and made accessible via the Internet. With your connected computer you order home the Web pages that you want to look at in your Web browser. E-mail is another utilization of the Internet. E-letters are sent between different mail servers which are connected to the Internet. File transfer is a third usage of the Internet.

The foundation of the Internet was a network in the US that connected defences and universities. Up to the 1990's the main users were the researchers who worked at research establishments and universities. In the 1990's, the Web caught on and the Internet became increasingly commercialized. In the 21st century the Internet has become a natural part of many people's everyday life and is no longer seen as something strange.

Web addresses

A Web address is called a URL (Uniform Resource Locator). Each URL is unique and leads to a specific file on a specific computer.

A URL is constructed according to the following:

http://www.omis.se/exempel/webb/webpage.html

http:// means that the Web browser uses the Hypertext Transfer Protocol (HTTP) to get the file to your computer. Other protocols are for example used for e-mail or file collecting.

www.omis.se is the name of the computer (often called a Web server) where the file (the Web page) is stored. The ending .se shows that it is a page which belongs to the Swedish top-level domain on the Internet.

/exempel/webb/ is the directory and sub-directory on the computer (the Web server) that the file (the Web page) is on.

webpage.html is the name of the file. The file ending .html shows that it is a page written in the Hypertext Markup Language (HTML).

Web addresses are thus structured according to the following:

how-to-get-there://where-to-go/what-to-collect

IP numbers

The IP number (the IP address) is the unique adress of the computer which makes communication on the Internet possible. The IP adress is controlled by the *Internet Protocol* (IP) and consists of 32 bits which are generally written decimally, e.g. 194.14.94.1. The DNS (*Domain Name System*) translates the domain in the Web address, e.g. www.omis.se, to an IP number so that communication can take place between the computers on the Internet via the protocol TCP/IP. (TCP/IP is a standard for computer communication which builds on the two protocols TCP and IP.)

Static Web pages

An ordinary "old-fashioned" Web page written in the HTML language and saved as a file on a Web server is a static Web page. The Web page is only altered if a new version of the file is uploaded to the Web server replacing the old one. Static Web pages are often created manually in a text-editing program or in a program with a graphical user interface such as Frontpage. The static pages contain general information as they have to be changed by hand. Most static Web pages are indexable, i.e. the search engines can add them to their databases. Problems may arise from *frames* or different scripts.

HTML

To know basic HTML is important to be able to use the search engines in an efficient way. The large search engines are originally constructed to manage only HTML pages, and many of their search features build on the different elements in, or parts of, the HTML.

A simple HTML page is shown below. The following pages contain an explanation to the HTML code for www.omis.se/exempel/webb/webpage.html.

Universities

Lund University (LU)

Stockholm University (SU)

Where do I find more Swedish universities?

Try to search with "university site:se" in a search engine like Google and Yahoo. Site:se limits the search to the Swedish domain .se, and thereby excludes hits from other domains like .no (Norway) or .edu (education in the US).

Search within a site or domain: [   ]

(e.g. youtube.com, .edu)

Picture. Box for site-search in Google..

In most search engines there are possibilities for limiting a search to a specific site or domain in "advanced search". The picture above shows the box in Google where the site can be specified.

Image. The Web page www.jonasfransson.com/example/webpage.html

The HTML code for the Web page in the image above:

```
<html>
<head>
<title>Web page</title>
</head>
<body>
<h1>Universities</h1>
<p><a href="http://www.lu.se/lund-university">Lund University (LU)</a></p>
<p><a href="http://www.su.se/english/">Stockholm University (SU)</a></p>
<br>
<h3>Where do I find more Swedish universities?</h3>
<p>Try to search with "university site:se" in a search engine like Google and
Yahoo. Site:se limits the search to the Swedish domain .se, and thereby ex-
cludes hits from other domains like .no (Norway) or .edu (education in the
US).</p>
<img src="google-site-box.png" alt="Box for limiting search to specific site or
domain in Google" border="0">
<p><i>Picture. Box for site-search in Google.</i>.</p>
<br>
<p>In most search engines there are possibilities for limiting a search to a
specific <b>site</b> or <b>domain</b> in "advanced search". The picture
above shows the box in Google where the site can be specified.</p>
```

```
</body>
</html>
```

The words within <> are called gags and could be said to be commands. In the first line it is decided that the document is an HTML document.

```
<html>
<head>
<title> Web page </title>
</head>
```

Then comes the head of the document (*head*) where the title of the document is given: "Web page". It's the title that is shown in the list at the top of the page in the Web browser. What it says in the head is not visible on the Web page itself but has other functions. After that the head is completed (/ inside the tags means that the command ends) and the "body" follows ", <body>. It's the text in the body that is shown in the Web browser's window.

```
<body>
<h1> Universities </h1>
```

h1 is a heading, the highest level which gives big headings.

```
<p><a href="http://www.lu.se/lund-university">Lund University (LU)</a></p>
<p><a href="http://www.su.se/english/">Stockholm University (SU)</a></p>
```

<p> means the beginning of a paragraph. The section consists of five paragraphs using the same structure and each paragraph contains a link to a daily paper. The link is structured according to the following:

```
<a href="http://www.lu.se/lund-university">Lund University (LU)</a>
```

a stands for *anchor*, which is the code for a link.

href=http://www.lu.se/lund-university is a hypertext reference which in this case leads to the English-speaking start page of Lund University.

Lund University (LU) is the clickable text.

/a means that the link is completed.

```
<br>
```

br stands for BREAK, i.e. a new line.

```
<h3>Where do I find more Swedish universities?</h3>
<p>Try to search with "university site:se" in a search engine like Google and
Yahoo. Site:se limits the search to the Swedish domain .se, and thereby ex-
cludes hits from other domains like .no (Norway) or .edu (education in the
US).</p>
```

The text above is a text section with a heading. The heading is of level 3, meaning that it's smaller than h1 above.

```
<img src="google-site-box.png" alt="Box for limiting search to specific site or
domain in Google" border="0">
<p><i>Picture. Box for site-search in Google.</i>.</p>
```

<img src> stands for *image source* and inserts an image with the name " google-site-box.png" on the page. Alt="…" is the text shown if you can't see the image for some reason, for example due to visual impairment. The tag determines the height and width of the image and whether it should have a frame. After that comes a paragraph with a caption in italics (<i>).

```
<p>In most search engines there are possibilities for limiting a search to a
specific <b>site</b> or <b>domain</b> in "advanced search". The picture
above shows the box in Google where the site can be specified.</p>
</body>
</html>
```

In the last section two words are marked with <b> for text in bold type (*bold*). The section and the whole example ends with the completion of the document body (*body* and after that the page ends with </html>.

Sometimes "&aring" and similar expressions occur in HTML text. &aring means "and a+ring", i.e. the Swedish "å". The paraphrases of language-specific signs are required for these to be correctly shown in all Web browsers

Meta tags

Meta tags are tags in the head of the HTML page where meta-information can be entered. Meta-information is information about information, e.g. who created the page. In the meta tags of a Web page, the page's creator can specify keywords and concepts under which the page will be located. The search engines can then consider the words in the meta tags at the relevance estimation. Earlier it was often information from the meta tags that was shown in the search engines' hit lists. Google was one of the first search engines to instead show excerpts from the Web page text in their hit list. However, meta tags is something which has been abused as pages have been given popular search words as tags in order to attract visitors, without the tags having had anything to do with the contents of the page. The importance of the meta tags for both page creators and visitors has diminished radically and today the large search engines pay little or no attention to the meta tags. In the cases where they actually consider the meta tags, the search engine checks the words in the meta tags against the text contents on the Web page of interest to be able to ignore meta tags which don't match the contents.

Dynamic Web pages

Dynamic pages are not, unlike the static pages, lying "ready" on a server. They are created from the different choices that you make when you visit a Web site. Sometimes the Web site remembers your choices, e.g. colour settings, and at that point the Web site uses so-called cookies (small filters that are saved on your computer).

With dynamic Web pages it's possible to create e-trade solutions, discussion forums and on-line journals.

The information (the contents) on the dynamic Web pages is saved in a database and when you visit a dynamic page a page is created for you from the information in the database and from the frames of the Web site. In certain cases the information is updated often, as for example the newspapers' front pages, and in that case the "age" of the information together with the news value is important.

One way of finding out whether a Web page is dynamic is to study its Web address (URL). If the URL contains a question mark in the middle, it is a sign of the page being a dynamic Web page.

Dynamically generated information can sometimes be hard to find in the search engines. It depends on the system through which the information is published, and how this system works, if the search engines will be able to find and enter the information into their indexes.

The Web browser

A Web browser is a program in your computer which makes it possible for you to see HTML documents and with that have access to all the information and all the files that are accessible via the Web. Today Microsoft's Internet Explorer is the most common Web browser, but others exist as well. Mozilla Firefox is an example of a new Web browser. Before Microsoft made Internet Explorer into a part of its operating system Windows, Netscape Navigator was the most common Web browser.

So-called plug-ins hook into the Web browser and these are small programs that improve the functionality of the Web browser. Many sound- and image files require that you have a certain plug-in to make them visible, or audible, in the Web browser. If you click on a link to a file that your Web browser doesn't support, a window will often pop up to ask you if you want to install the program referred to. Most of the programs are free of charge and safe to install on your computer if you follow the instructions.

With the Web browser you can manage the Web pages in different ways. You can save addresses (favourites/bookmarks), print Web pages, send the page or the link via e-mail, and also save the file to your computer.

Different types of search services

Search services are navigation tools on the Web. The search services don't in themselves contain any information, but links to pages with contents. The search services can be divided into three fundamentally different types:

- ◆ Search engines
- ◆ Directories

* Meta search services

Search engines

Search engines automatically index Web pages, i.e. computer programs read and save Web pages into a database. When you perform a search in a search engine you search in its database, not out on the Web. Examples are Google (google.com) and Yahoo! search (search.yahoo.com).

Directories

Directories are created by human beings, in contrast to the search engines. The editors, often librarians, collect links and place them in a hierarchy of subjects. Usually the links are commented and sometimes labelled with subject words. Examples are the Librarians' Internet Index (lii.org) and Infoo (http://infoo.se/index-en.html).

Meta search services

Meta search services are search services that perform searches in other search services, in directories and search engines, and which then put together a hit list. In some meta search services advertising is mixed in with the hit list. Examples are Clusty (clusty.com) and Metacrawler (metacrawler.com).

Operation and financing of search services

The search services differ from each other with regard to operation and financing. They play in different divisions and have different origins and purposes. They can be divided into the following categories (examples within parenthesis):

* Non-profit work (e.g. the Open Directory Project)
* Hobby (individual persons' link collections)
* Advertising (e.g. Google)
* PR for a special search technique or company (e.g. the Bright Planet)
* Publicly financed search service (e.g. Librarians' Internet Index)
* Research project (many of the search engines started as research projects, e.g. Google)

Terminology

There is no clear terminology on search services. I use search services as the comprehensive concept under which I place three types: search engines, directories and meta search services. But the word search engines is often used to refer to all search services. In computer science a search engine, however, is the part of for example Google which performs the search in the index, not the whole search service (i.e. yet a more narrow definition). Other concepts are search machines or search robots.

When it comes to directory services there are yet more concepts: directories, or catalogues (plus subject- or Web directories), link lists, link collections, portals/ subject portals (or gateways) and virtual libraries.

Database

I use the concept database for a limited amount of information which is stored in a structured system that is accessible through a specific interface. The databases often contain information in a narrow subject. Databases in this sense have existed long before the Web and they have been accessible via cd-rom, modems etc. Now most of them are reachable via the Internet through Web interfaces, but many of them require registration or subscription.

Beta version

A beta version is a version of a computer program or a Web service which is under development. The program or the service might not be entirely stable and as a user you can't place the same requirements on a beta version. Beta versions are often marked by the addition *beta* after the name. Beta versions are particularly common when it comes to new Web services.

2. Search Engines

Search engines is the type of search services mostly used. To seek information via Google has even become a verb—to google. To google has come to mean a search through a search engine, not just on Google. The largest search engines are:

* Google (www.google.com)
* Yahoo! (http://search.yahoo.com)
* Bing (www.bing.com), formerly Live Search and MSN

What really is a search engine?

A search engine is a search service which automatically indexes Web pages and, to some extent, other file types. Search engines are computer programs which read Web pages on the Internet and store these in a database. When you make a search, the search engine searches its database for relevant material which it then presents to you.

To enter one or a couple of search words in the search box in Google is not that difficult, so what's the point of trying to understand how a search engine works? If you want to get a bit more out of your search, want to search more efficiently or get more exact hits, you'll need an understanding of how a search engine works. Also, with a deeper knowledge of search engines comes the understanding of what you may expect from search engines and how unlike search engines may be, both technically and in practice. It's not at all a given that they will index the same things or that they rank or present sponsored links in the same way. When you realize the weaknesses of the search engines you'll understand the strengths of the other search services. Last but not least, you'll need certain knowledge of how search engines work to understand what the Invisible Web is, all of that which isn't included by the search engines.

How does a search engine work?

A large search engine like Google is a complex system which consists of thousands of computers. In order for the user to get a good idea of how a search engine works, you can divide it into three parts:

* **The Spider** – finds and collects Web pages
* **The Indexer** – indexes and stores Web pages
* **The Query Processor** – delivers search results

The Spider

The spider follows and collects links. Before you can find the information in the search engine the search engine itself has to find it. The spider is a small program that is constantly "on the net" to find new pages for the search engine to index, that is, to store in the database. The spider works more or less in the same way as you and I when we're surfing. It follows links that it finds and the Web pages are downloaded to the search engine (we do the same thing in our Web browser). The new downloaded Web pages, the addresses, are sent to the indexer where they are placed in a queue for indexing. The spider does not only find new Web pages, it regularly revisits the pages that already exist in the search engine's index in order to keep its database updated.

Two things distinguish the spider from you and your Web browser. The spider can follow links backwards, that is, it can follow links that lead to a page, not only links that lead from it. The spider can also download thousands of pages at once, not only one at a time as we have to do.

How do the search engines find the Web pages? A new search engine is "fed" with an address list to existing Web sites. After that the spider requests the Web pages in the list and sends them on to the indexer, but at the same time it looks for links to other Web pages. If it finds links to other pages these are added to the spider's visit list. It is also possible to register the address to one's Web site on some search engines in order for the search engine to find and index it. When it comes to revisits to already indexed pages, the spider's point of departure is the addresses which exist in the index.

The spider is also called *robot, bot, web crawler* or *crawler*.

The Indexer

The indexer is the part that fetches the Web pages, divides them and stores them in the index (the database). The index stores information indicating on what Web page each word can be found and where on the page it is found; the information is stored irrespective of if it concerns common text, headings, captions (the so-called ALT tag) or links. The index of the search engines is constructed in the same way as the index that you find at the very end of a book. Each word refers to the pages where they can be found.

The size of the index is an important competitiveness factor between the different search engines. Bigger is often better. But at the time of writing, the major search engines indexes contain over 20 billion indexed pages, probably over 100 billion pages. A couple of years ago the search engines declared their index size on their home pages, but now they occasionally mention a number in a press release. But it is hard to compare the figures because the search engines counts in different ways.

Certain search engines, among others Google, store a copy of the indexed Web page. It's the copy that you get to see if you choose the link Cached in Google's hit list. If the real Web page is not accessible for the time being, the cached page might be a way out. But the cached page may be far from updated. Several months might have passed since the search engine last indexed the Web page. Sometimes there is a date on the cached page and then you know when the search engine visited the page last time.

The Query Processor

The query processor is the part that you as a searcher meet. It processes the query (your search words), calculates relevance and presents the results (that is, it creates a hit list for exactly your query). It's this part of the search engine that differs most between the various search engines. Each search engine has a unique (and secret) way of determining the relevance and of creating hit lists. Some people claim that this is why Google has become so popular, the users experience that they get good hit lists in response to their searches. At the same time, Google was the first one to use a clean and publicity-free search page (a fact which is also used to explain Google's popularity).

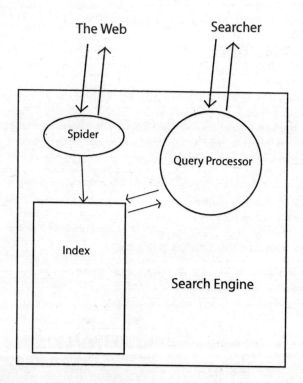

Fig. The structure of search engines

Different programming

All three parts of the search engine may be programmed in different ways. Examples:

- The spider prioritizes certain links above others when it collects links.
- The indexer does not enter all the information on the Web page, perhaps only the first 100 lines or a certain amount of kilobytes. Google earlier indexed 101 kb and Yahoo! 500 kb.
- The way the query processor calculates the relevance is a determining difference between the search engines.

As the owner makes all these selections at the programming of the search engine, each search engine becomes unique with its own behaviour, strengths and weaknesses. If you try to use two or three search engines regularly, you'll get to know them and will be able to use their strengths. And you'll realize how different they are.

Examples of rules at the collection and indexation of links.

- The search engine revisits pages according to a certain schedule. Popular pages are visited daily, while obscure and odd pages may never be revisited.
- Certain types of pages are difficult or impossible to "crawl," for example pages with frames or a difficult coding (today all large search engines index frames).
- A Webmaster may use the possibility to prevent the spider from visiting or indexing certain defined pages (robots.txt or the meta tag robots).
- Certain search engines remove pages from the database, among other things due to lack of room.

You can analyse how a Web page works in relation to a search engine spider.

The search engine Seekport (www.seekport.co.uk) has a service, Seekbot, where you can analyse how a specific page works in relation to the search engine's spider.

The inverted index of the search engines

The search engines store the indexed Web pages in an inverted index. The index contains references to the pages on which the search word can be found

Example of inverted index

The search engine has indexed 32 pages and the word *amazon* is found on the pages 2, 7, 11, 12 and 30. *Volvo*, however, is found on the pages 4, 8, 12, 15 and 24

The index looks more or less like this:
amazon 2, 7, 11, 12, 30
volvo 4, 8, 12, 15, 24

A search for:
amazon gives the pages: 2, 7, 11, 12, 30
volvo gives the pages: 4, 8, 12, 15, 24
amazon OR volvo gives the pages: 2, 4, 7, 8, 11, 12, 15, 24, 30
amazon AND volvo gives the page: 12

The concepts OR and AND are described further in Chapter 8 which deals with search techniques.

How relevance/ranking is determined

The search engines' ranking is determined in a similar way, but each one has its own secret formula. A large number of factors are balanced against each other in a way that is unique to the search engine and from this balancing a hit list is created. Most of the factors concern the search words, as for example how many times the word can be found on the different pages. The search engines also look at the number of people who link to the respective page and from where the links are coming. Common factors are:

Number of occurrences (word frequency)

If the search word occurs 30 times in a document, this document probably deals more with the subject in demand than a document in which the word is only mentioned once.

Occurrences/document size (word density)

If the search words occurs 20 times in a document of 1000 words, this document probably deals more with the subject than if the search word occurs 20 times in a document of 10 000 words.

Overall rareness of the search word (inverse document frequency)

This is a way of measuring the importance of a word. The fewer times a word occurs in the database (the document collection), the more important or unique is the word.

Nearness (proximity)

In searches of more words, a shorter distance between the search words in the document is generally a sign of higher relevance.

Where the search word is found

If a word is found in the document title or file name it's likely that the document to a greater extent deals with the subject than a document with a different name. This also applies if the word is found in headings, the first section, captions, etc. Sometimes the word is only found in the links to the page, not on the actual page, and it may be confusing when you don't find your search word on the pages in the hit list.

Link popularity

How many users follow the different links? Link popularity is nothing that the search engines talk about today, partly because the development goes towards more "scientific" calculation methods. Earlier the link popularity constituted a more important factor in the relevance calculation, but all search engines probably take it into some consideration.

Link analysis

Which are the "characteristics" of the link? Where does it come from? How is the link described in the link text? One example is Google's PageRank (see below), but all large search engines analyse links.

Google's PageRank

PageRank (PR) is the name of Google's link analysis. When Google was launched in 1998 they were the first to use a more advanced link analysis. Today all large search engines operate in a similar way.

The basis of PageRank is:

♦ The Web page quality can be assessed by the number of links to the page.

♦ Incoming links to a page are more important than the outgoing links from the page. (A sort of citation analysis).

With the two points above as starting points, a calculation system has been created to obtain the weight of a Web page, that is, to measure how important it is in relation to the rest of the Web.

Google describes the method on their Web page:[1]

"PageRank reflects our view of the importance of web pages by considering more than 500 million variables and 2 billion terms. Pages that we believe are important pages receive a higher PageRank and are more likely to appear at the top of the search results.

PageRank also considers the importance of each page that casts a vote, as votes from some pages are considered to have greater value, thus giving the linked page greater value. We have always taken a pragmatic approach to help improve search quality and create useful products, and our technology uses the collective intelligence of the web to determine a page's importance."

In practice this means that a link from a big and famous Web site (with a high PR) is more important than many links from unknown pages (with a low PR). Link analysis and PageRank improvement is one of the fields that so-called search engine optimisation consultants work with in order to improve a Web page's placement on the hit list (see further in Chapter 10).

---

1 Google - Corporate Information - Technology Overview: www.google.com/intl/en/corporate/tech.html (2009-06-25)

In the Google Toolbar, PR is shown as a number between 0 and 10 for the Web pages that you visit. In Google Directory, the PR is shown in the form of a small meter (www.google.com/dirhp). The PR is, actually, a logarithmic value (like the Richter scale) between 0 and 1.

Ranking in Google

But at a search the PR is merely one of the many variables that are balanced against others before the placement on the hit list is determined. The balancing is done by means of the search engine's secret algorithm. The calculation is secret as each search engine wants to offer the most relevant hit list to the users (and gain market shares). The algorithm is also secret to prevent outsiders from manipulating their own Web site to obtain a high placement on the hit list. If you understand how, for example, Google calculates its ranking you can create a Web site using your knowledge of how the search engine works and with that ignore the relevance calculation.

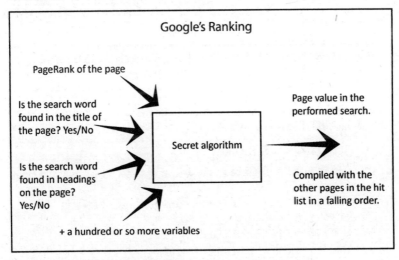

Fig. Illustration of Google's ranking.

The figure of Google's ranking illustrates the many variables that are balanced against each other in the secret algorithm. PageRank is only one of many variables, but only Google knows how important it is in practice.

The balance between the different parts done by means of the secret algorithm changes somewhat all the time, partly as a result of the above mentioned reasons, partly as a result of improvement and the act of keeping it a secret.

Google gives the following steps to describe a search in its search engine:

1. Search in the index for all the pages that contain the search words.

2. Relevance analysis of the found pages through examining where and how often the search words occur.

3. Assessment of the reputation of the Web sites, that is, an analysis of those that link to respective Web site, where the found pages are, to obtain applicability/popularity. Google calls this assessment PageRank (PR).

4. The Web pages are ranked by adding together relevance (step 2) and reputation (step 3) and after that Google produces a hit list based on the calculated applicability.

The process in the search engines is the same, so the description above could be said to apply to just any search engine.

Myths about search engines

There are many myths about search engines. The most common are:

The search engines search on the net

The search engines do not search on the net, they search in the database (index) that they have created from Web pages. The size of the index of the different search engines are important because web pages that are not in the index will not show up in the hit lists.

All search engines are the same

They vary substantially in many respects:

- The size (how large the index is).
- Updating of the index.
- Coverage of the Web.
- They have different "personalities", strengths/weaknesses and advantages/disadvantages.
- How they process search inquiries.
- The presentation of the results (the ranking).

All together this means that the search engines are not alike. At a search for a specific Web site, i.e. the government's site, the differences will not be noticed since all, probably, will place the link to this Web site at the very top of the hit list. But for most other searches you'll gain from searching in several different search engines.

The indexes of the search engines are updated

The indexes of the search engines are not entirely updated for various reasons:

- Crawling the Web is expensive as computer power is needed.
- More popular pages are re-indexed more frequently just because they get visits more often, while less effort is given to less popular Web sites.

- An older page on a Web site is indexed, but the link in the search engine leads to a new page since the older page has been altered or replaced since the indexing.

If you choose cached in Google or cached page in Bing it will tell you when the stored page was last visited.

The coverage of the different search engines overlap

How big the overlap is between the large search engines is a matter of discussion. What applies is generally this:

- The overlap of the large search engines is much greater when it comes to much frequented, popular Web pages than obscure, seldom visited pages.

- The overlap in the index is larger than the overlap in the hit lists as the search engines calculate relevance in different ways.

- If you search for popular subjects you don't have to think so much about the search engine's coverage, but if you search for unusual subjects you should use several search engines for the search.

The index of the search engines is extensive

- The large search engines cover 5-10 % of the visible Web (no one knows for sure and it depends on how you count).

- The search engines can't keep up with the explosive growth of the Web.

- The search engines can't find all pages on the Web (some pages don't have any links leading to or from the page).

- Each search engine has its own rules that it follows for collecting and indexing pages.

The size of the index is a piece of information kept within the walls of the search-engine companies. Occasionally a search engine will make a statement saying that they have now indexed x billion pages. Google, Bing and Yahoo! have more than 20 billion, maybe more than 100 billion, pages in their indexes at the time of writing (May 2009).

When should you use a search engine?

Some guidelines for when to use a search engine are listed below. In Chapter 5 you'll find more advice on the choice of search service.

- When you are searching for an exclusive or odd subject.
- When you are searching for a specific Web site.
- When you want to find particular document types, for example PDF files.
- When you want to search the full text of many pages.
- When you want to find many documents in your subject.

Specialized search engines

Specialized search engines have their own indexes but are directed in different ways, that is, they don't index "everything" as the large search engines do. The limitations result in these search engines becoming more focused and in their capacity to index more material. Sometimes specialized search engines are called vertical search engines.

Subject

The subject orientation may be everything from science to recipes. One example is Scirus (www.scirus.com) which indexes scientific material.

Service

The focus may be blogs or news sites. Google blog search (http://blogsearch. google.com) is one example of a blog search engine.

File type

Search engines can be limited to particular file types such as PDF files or MP3. One example is the Adobe PDF search (http://searchpdf.adobe.com).

See further in search service collections, e.g.:

- ◆ Search Engine Colossus (www.searchenginecolossus.com)
- ◆ Beaucoup (www.beaucoup.com)
- ◆ Google Directory: Computers > Internet > Searching > Search Engines > Specialized (http://directory.google.com)

Compare hit lists

Thumbshots.com has a useful service which compares the first hundred hits for different searches in a few search engines – Thumbshots Ranking (http://ranking. thumbshots.com).

The significance of the order of the search words at a search on Google is shown below. A reversal of the two search words produces different hit lists. Each marked dot in the two lines is a hit found in both hit lists. The lines between the marked dots show where the corresponding hit is found in the other hit list. Unmarked dots are unique hits for the hit list.

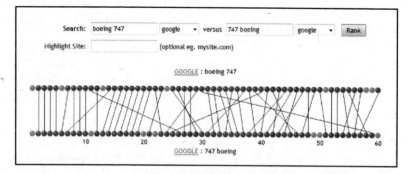

Fig. Comparison between "boeing 747" and "747 boeing" on Google

In the search above, barely 7 of the 60 hits are unique, i.e., the overlap is 88 per cent. Among the ten first hits the ranking corresponds fairly well, but further down in the hit lists the differences become bigger. Hit 1 is unique in the two searches, which is remarkable.

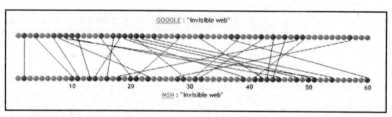

Fig. Search on the "Invisible Web"on Google and Live (MSN).

The search engines have different ways of ranking the hits. Above you find a search on the *"Invisible Web"* on Google and Live (MSN). Only 42 per cent of the first sixty hits in respective hit list overlap between the two search engines.

Precision and recall

At a search there are two standards of how efficient a search or a search service is, *recall* and *precision*. In a given quantity of documents, a certain number of them are relevant to a specific query. But far from always these exact documents are retrieved.

Each search gives a number of retrieved documents, where some of them are relevant, i.e. the overlapping between relevant and retrieved documents in the figure above.

Precision refers to the number of overlapping documents divided by the number of retrieved documents. The precision should preferably be high as the retrieved documents in this case contain few irrelevant documents.

Recall refers to the number of overlapping documents divided by the number of relevant documents. When the recall is high, a large number of the relevant documents have been retrieved.

Preferably both precision and recall should be high as the search engine then delivers practically only relevant hits and, at the same time, all the relevant hits in its index. But in practice, and to a certain extent, precision and recall cancel each other out. If the number of hits is increased at a search (higher recall), it means that the number of irrelevant hits also increases (lower precision).

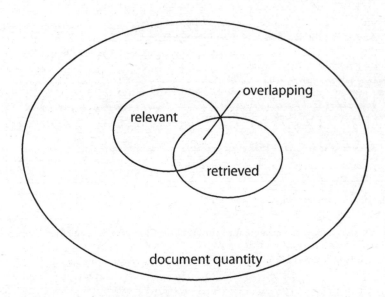

Fig. Document quantity with relevant documents, retrieved documents and overlapping.

As a standard, recall is perhaps not entirely relevant for Web searches as most users only look at the first hits in the hit list. The fact that a search gives eleven thousand hits may not be interesting. On the contrary, it would probably stress us out as searchers if we knew that all the hits in the Google search were relevant to our search.

When searching on the Web, precision is so much more important, particularly for the first hits on the first pages of the hit list, the pages that one really looks at.

3. Directories

About directory services

The directory could be called the human search service as it's the only one of the three search service types that is created and maintained by humans.

Three types of directories can be distinguished:

- General directories
- Subject directories
- Link collections

Principally it's the size and direction that set them apart. The general directories are large, attempting to cover all subjects. The major general directories on the Net contain about 5 million links. The subject directories are, as the name suggests, concentrated on different subjects. The subject directories often have an academic focus, and their size can vary a lot. The link collections can be constituted by small collections of links that private persons have put together. But link collections are also often produced by different institutions or interest groups.

The character of directory services

Common for the directories is that they are *organized* and *selective*.

Organized because people have collected and structured the links, in contrast to the search engines which do everything automatically. Sometimes the links are also commented and labelled with subject words. Major directories have a hierarchical structure in which each subject has a given place. At times the subject hierarchy follows one of the library systems, e.g. the Swedish SAB system by which many libraries are arranged. Really high-class directories also have a standardized vocabulary, i.e. in the description of the links specific expressions and phrases are used to make them easier to find.

Selective because the links are chosen among many other links. Professional directory services publish their selection criteria so that everyone may know about them. You find more about the contents below.

Directory contents

To create and maintain a directory is demanding work. The maintenance work is often underrated which is why it's neglected which, in turn, leads to the directory becoming obsolete. To minimize the maintenance work links which meet the criteria listed below are often chosen:

- Well-written
- Possess quality
- Created by authoritative originators
- Stable (not likely to move or change contents)
- Updated

The link to the Swedish Government (www.regeringen.se) is very stable. The URL (the Web address) will probably be the same as long as the Web looks like it does today. For that reason directory editors often choose links to top-level pages (such as www.omis.se) and not links to pages far down in the structure, (for example www.omis.se/uppladdat/kurser/lub/lub-lankar.html). It's much likelier that the later one will be changed or disappears, while the link to the top-level page normally is the last one to disappear.

When should you choose a directory?

- When you need to do a search for a broad subject or a broad idea.
- When you want to get a list with Web sites that are recommended or commented by experts.
- When you don't want to look through a lot of documents that are not relevant.

General directories

Examples of general directories:

- Open Directory (http://dmoz.org)
- Yahoo! (http://dir.yahoo.com)
- Librarians' Internet Index (http://lii.org)

Universal subject structure

The large directories are general in regard to their contents and their structure builds on a "universal" subject structure. The subject structure in the general directories covers all conceivable subjects. Generally they have between 10 and 25 top categories and then follow large quantities of sub-categories.

The SAB system as an example of a universal subject structure

The SAB system is the most common classification system in Swedish libraries. The system was created in the beginning of the 20th century, just like many of the other library classification systems, and it reflects the time of its creation. One example of this is that the military system has been given a letter of its own, S, while economics and trade on Q covers everything from national economics to cookery books and cooking.

SAB	Subject
A	Books and libraries
B	General
C	Religion
D	Philosophy and Psychology
E	Children and Education
F	Linguistics
G	Literary History
H	Poetry and Fiction
J	Archaeology
K	History
L	Biography and Genealogy
M	Ethnography, Social Anthropology, Ethnology
N	Geography and Local History
O	Social Sciences and Law
P	Technology, Manufacturing and Transport
Q	Economics, Trade and Industry
R	Sports and Games
S	Military and Naval Systems
T	Mathematics
U	Science
V	Medicine
X	Sheet Music

Fig. The SAB system which is used in many Swedish libraries

All categories are divided into sub-categories. Category E, Children and Education, is divided into four blocks:

Ea—Eh	Pedagogy
Em—Eu	Educational System
Ev	Adult Education
Ex	Choice of Education

Fig. Division of Children and Education (E) in the SAB system.

A letter or letter combination is called a signum. In the SAB system, one or several subject words are linked to each signum.

On the Web site of the National Library of Sweden you can do searches using different subject words and thus obtain the SAB codes. Or you can do a search using the SAB codes and get the subject words (www.kb.se/bibliotek/amnesord/sok-index/).

The Librarians' Internet Index (LII), http://lii.org, has a different subject structure (see below).

Arts & Humanities History, Literature and Books, Music, more	**Media** Magazines, News, Newspapers, more
Business Finance, Industries, Jobs, more	**People** Families, Gay and Lesbian, Notable People, more
Computers Internet, Technology, Web Design and Management, more	**Recreation** Crafts, Hobbies, Sports, Travel, more
Government Military, Politics, Taxes, more	**Reference** Dictionaries, Holidays, more
Health Diseases and Conditions, Drugs, Nutrition, more	**Regional** California, Washington, The World, more
Home and Housing Consumer Research & Advocacy, Food & Cooking, Gardening, more	**Science** Astronomy, Biology, Environment, more
Law Civil Liberties, Crime, Treaties, more	**Society & Social Science** Charities/Nonprofits, Education, Ethics, Religion, more

Fig. The universal subject structure in LII.

The entries in the LII are ambitiously set up with descriptive texts and information about when the entry was created, by whom and when it was last modified. Each entry also has subject words according to the Library of Congress Subject Headings (LCSH), a US system run by the Library of Congress in Washington. To get more information about the entry you click on the magnifying glass after the heading.

Fig. Entries in lii.org on "vikings" in the category of History

The placing of a subject in the hierarchy of subjects is not a given, but differs between the various directory services, see the example below.

The example of opera in different directories

Yahoo! directory	Entertainment > Music > Genres > Classical > Opera
Open directory	Arts > Music > Styles > O > Opera
Internet Public Library	Arts & Humanities > Fine Arts > Performing Arts > Music > Opera

The construction of directories

Directory services are created and maintained in different ways. You find one division between open and closed directories. The open directories are constructed by voluntaries, while the closed ones are run by a smaller group of salaried editors. The Open Directory (http://dmoz.org) is an open directory to which anyone can sign up for participation.

Examples of closed directories are commercial directories such as Yahoo! (http://dir.yahoo.com) and About (www.about.com), but also publicly funded directory services such as the Librarians' Internet Index (http://lii.org).

Subject directories

Subject directories are directories that limit themselves to a subject area or to a type of resources, e.g. academic resources. Subject directories often focus on one academic area.

An example of a subject directory is Infomine (http://infomine.ucr.edu) from the US which contains large quantities of academic resources in different subjects.

Subject directories can have many names and come in many shapes. They can be called *subject-based Internet gateways, subject gateways, subject portals* or *vortals* (from vertical portal). And under the denomination "links" many things may be concealed.

The subject directories can be hard to find, particularly as they often constitute a minor part of the Web site of an interest group or a special library, perhaps hidden under the term "links". If you only find them, navigation tools on the Web are among the most important instruments an information seeker can have.

Link collections

Link collections are often quite small and often have just one editor. The contents are entirely dependent upon the editor's subject interest and the will to keep the collection updated. Link collections seldom have any explicit quality requirements. But for information seekers link collections may be valuable, if you find a collection dealing with your subject.

CHILDREN'S RIGHTS

Main Standards and Mechanisms

Instruments

United Nations

Declaration of the Rights of the Child
Proclaimed by General Assembly resolution 1386(XIV) of 20 November 1959
Convention on the Rights of the Child
Adopted and opened for signature, ratification and accession by General Assembly resolution 44/25 of 20 November 1989 entry into force 2 September 1990, in accordance with article 49.

- Status of ratifications
- Ratification and Reservations
- General measures of implementation for the Convention on the Rights of the Child
  03/10/2003. CRC/GC/2003/5. (General Comments)

Optional Protocol to the Convention on the Rights of the Child on the sale of children, child prostitution and child pornography
Adopted and opened for signature, ratification and accession by General Assembly resolution A/RES/54/263 of 25 May 2000 enters into force on 18 January 2002

- Status Ratifications
- Declarations and Reservations

Optional Protocol to the Convention on the Rights of the Child on the involvement of children in armed conflicts

- Status of Ratifications
- Declarations and Reservations

Fig. Children's Rights links from the Raoul Wallenberg Institute of Human Rights and Humanitarian Law library (http://www.rwi.lu.se/library/childrens.shtml)

More directories

Many directories are hard to classify. Some usable directories follow here below:

- Intute (www.intute.ac.uk)
- BUBL Link (http://bubl.ac.uk) (classifies according to Dewey)

Searching in directories

Searching in the subject structure

The subject structure is often easy to find and there are often references between sub-categories further down in the structure (often designated with @). Some directories are structured according to a library system, e.g. the Swedish SAB system or the US Dewey system.

Searching with search words

The directories often offer search possibilities, generally through a search box. When it comes to searching in directories you have to consider that you only search within the directory, on the links and the comments. You don't search on the contents of the linked pages, like you do in a search engine. Therefore you have to pick your search words with care and only do searches using one or two words.

What to consider regarding directories

Size

How many entries or links does the directory contain?

Policy

Does the directory have a published policy about quality- and selection criteria?

Biased coverage

What about the subject of the directory? The many resources on computers and programming may be seen as reflecting a bias on the Web.

Updating

Is the directory updated? The updating is often done slowly as it requires a manual control of each link.

Paid links

Is payment required for inclusion of links in the directory? There are directories that make a living by demanding payment for inclusion of links in the directory. And then we're not far from pure advertising services like the Yellow Pages.

Supplementary links

Many commercial directories bring in supplementary links from a partner (a search engine). Consider the differences regarding search possibilities between a directory and a search engine (in practice the search takes place in a partner search engine).

Social bookmark services

New forms of directory service are the social bookmark services, also called *social bookmark managers*. A social bookmark manager is a Web site where you can save links and search among the bookmarks that other users have saved. The saved bookmarks are always accessible on the Web (unless you choose to make them private). The bookmark services generally allow you to provide the bookmarks with subject words, normally called *tagging*. The tags are unchecked subject words that each user picks individually, in contrast to the supervised subject words from subject word lists or thesauruses used in databases and certain directory services.

The largest social bookmark services are:

♦   Blinklist – www.blinklist.com
♦   Delicious – http://delicious.com
♦   Diigo – www.diigo.com

Comments are sometimes saved together with the tags. The comments can give a hint as to what other users think about the Web site to which the actual bookmark leads. Some of the bookmark services also use grading of the bookmarks which can also be helpful when you're searching.

Popular tags are often presented in a *tag cloud* where more frequently used words are shown in bigger font and perhaps in a different colour. The font size depends entirely upon the usage of a tag. The result is not always correct as *blog* is distinguished from *blogs* and *web2.0* from *web 2.0* (with a space). But it's a good tool to rapidly get a general view or to choose the used tag. All tags in the cloud link to all the bookmarks with the tag. In the figure below, *design* and *blog* are the most used tags.

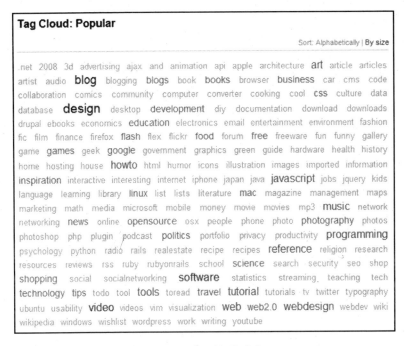

Fig. The most popular tags as a tag cloud in Delicious.

In contrast to other search services, the social bookmark services build on popularity and up-to-dateness. Popular bookmarks are listed for each tag and popular links are bookmarked by still more people.

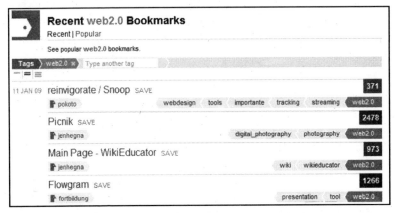

Fig. Popular bookmarks tagged with web2.0 on Delicious.

The figure above presents the most popular bookmarks for the tag web2.0 for the moment. The most recently bookmarked links for each tag are also often shown.

Sometimes tags closely related to the tag you have clicked on are shown. This may provide an easy way of getting closer to resources in the subject you're looking for. The closely related tags to web2.0 in Delicious are shown below.

Fig. Related tags to web2.0 in Delicious.

The search possibilities vary as much of the usage builds on the tags. Generally you can click on a user name and get the bookmarks that this user has put up with a specific tag. For example, in Delicious active users are listed under closely related tags for each tag. Through studying that which the great taggers have bookmarked you can find both good and updated Web sites which you would probably not have found otherwise.

How social bookmark services are used for the storage of links is described in Chapter 14.

4. Meta Search Services

Meta search services are search services that do searches in other search services in order to put together a hit list of their own. The meta search services often do searches in both search engines and directories. In many cases sponsored links are mixed into the hit list in an unclear way.

Some people mean that meta search services, or meta search engines as they are often called, is a variant of search engines. But for information seekers, the meta search services differ in several decisive ways from the search engines.

Important differences regarding:

- opportunities for advanced search possibilities
- where the links come from
- the way in which the hit list has been put together
- how commercial links are presented.

Get advanced search possibilities

The meta search services generally don't contain particularly advanced search possibilities. The searching can't be limited at all as it can be in a common search engine. This depends upon the fact that the meta search service does searches in many different search engines and directories, and the meta search service doesn't adapt its searches to the different search services to any great extent. Certain adaptation takes place, but largely the meta search service only mediates your search words to the other search services and collects the top results.

The origin of the links

The meta search services don't have indexes of their own but use those of others. They send queries to several search engines and directories at the same time. The meta search service then puts together the reported results into a hit list of its own. More frequently now it's shown where the links come from, but not always. It's not at all certain that the meta search service does searches in the largest search engines such as Google, Yahoo! and Bing.

A problem with the meta search services is that as they search in common search services, such as Google och Yahoo!, they also bring in hits from search engines that use only bought hits. The ordinary hits are then mixed with the bought hits in the hit list of the meta search service without any indication.

The way the hit list is put together

Generally the meta search service brings in rather few hits from the search services in which it searches, 10-20 hits is common. So even if the search generates several hundreds of hits in an ordinary search engine, the meta search service will only present the first tens of hits. When the search service has received the results from the search, a simple list is created. The hits from the large search engines are often weighted higher than the hits from smaller, unknown search services. Sometimes the hit list shows where the hit comes from and which place it had in respective search engine. If the hit is found in the results from several search services it will be placed higher up in the hit list.

But the hit lists can have many different appearances. They can be compiled or separate, i.e. one for each search service that the meta search service uses for searching. Some services use advanced technique, such as automatic clustering or categorization of the documents. The links in the hit list are then also divided into different sub-groups, different clusters, to facilitate the finding of relevant links.

Duplicates are normally removed from the hit list, and many of the modern meta search services bring together the duplicates and give them a higher ranking as they are found in the results from several search services. But in older and simpler meta search services duplicates sometimes occur in the hit lists.

The meta search services bring in a maximum number of hits from the search services. They interrupt the searching in the search services after a certain amount of time to prevent the search time period from getting too long which is why the maximum number of hits from all individual search services is not always reached. Some meta search services allow for a certain extent of regulation of the number of hits from each search service and the maximum search time period.

How commercial links are presented

Sponsored links are in many cases mixed into the hit list in an unclear way.

In the Metacrawler (www.metacrawler.com) search shown below the hits 1, 2, 3, 5, 6 and 7 are sponsored links. At first sight this is easy to miss as the hits are numbered normally, an ordinary link and a regular text snippet below the link. But under that it says "sponsored by" before the URL and the hit comes from "Ads by Google".

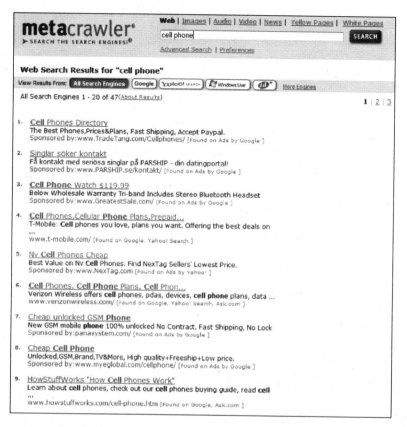

Fig. Searching in Metacrawler on "cell phone"

Most meta search services are commercial and run by means of advertising revenues. The services without advertising are research projects, publicly funded services or services run as the marketing of a specific search technology.

Searching in meta search services

To bear in mind regarding meta search services

- ♦ Which search services does the meta search service use for its searches? Try to find a list or do a search and study the hit list.

- ♦ They often perform only simple searches, they don't use any advanced search functions in the search engines.

41

- The number of hits from each search service is strictly limited (often 10-30 hits/search service).

Advantages with meta search services
- Useful when you only want a limited number of relevant hits.
- Good choice for obscure subjects.
- Suitable for testing when you don't find what you're looking for.
- Good for getting a survey of the things that exist on the Web in your subject.
- The hits in the hit list can be very relevant as they present the highest ranked hits in each search service used.

Disadvantages with meta search services
- Normally only simple queries, no advanced search possibilities.
- Often no field searching.
- Only gives the top hits in each search service, thus not representing the total results from any search service.

When is it suitable to use a meta search service?

- In the beginning of a search in an unfamiliar subject to get an idea of relevant search words and important resources.
- When you quickly want to get an overview of central Web pages in a subject.
- At searches with clearly delimited and exact queries.
- When you want a fast result on a simple or popular search using one or two search words.
- If you want to compare the query results between different search services quickly.

See Chapter 5 for further advice and suggestions regarding the choice of search service.

Different meta search services

Horizontal presentation of the hit list

Most search services present the results in a long vertical hit list, but some services present the results horizontally, in various sub-groups or clusters. This makes it easier for you as a seeker to zoom in on the aspects that are important to you.

The meta search service Clusty (www.clusty.com) groups the hits in different clusters. Through the clustered results different aspects of the search are rapidly obtained. To the left in the illustration below the different clusters for the search on "information seeking behavior" are shown. Out of the 187 hits 30 belong to the cluster "Research" and 17 to "Needs". If you want to get at a particular aspect, you click on the link for the cluster and the hits will show up in the hit list.

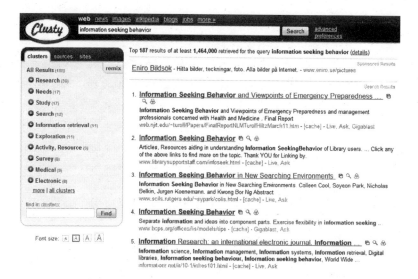

Fig. Hit list on Clusty from a search on "information seeking behavior".

In the ordinary hit list to the right you can see from which search services the link comes. In this example the first hit comes from Ask, Gigablast and Live (Bing). After the URL (the Web address) there is a nicety — "show in clusters"— through which you can see in which clusters the hit is included. And you can choose "new window" and "preview".

Graphic hit lists

Several meta search services present the hits in maps instead of in traditional lists.

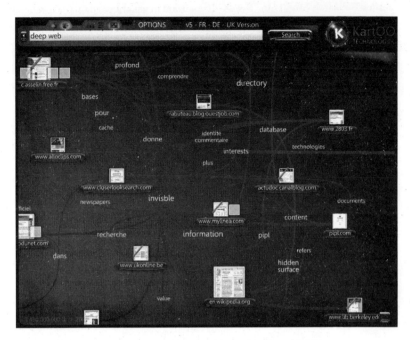

Fig. KartOO's chart with hits from a search on the "Deep Web".

Kartoo (www.kartoo.com) is a French meta search service that presents its hits graphically. The graphic presentation may be difficult to interpret in the beginning, but it can often give new aspects to the search. The hits are presented in different maps. Below to the right on the screen is a button, "next map", which leads to the next map.

Table of common meta search services

Meta search service	Searches in the following search services	Special features
Clusty (Vivisimo) http://clusty.com	Bing (Live), Ask, Gigablast, Open Directory	Clusters the results.
Dogpile www.dogpile.com	Google, Yahoo!, Bing, Ask	All four large search engines.
Ixquick www.ixquick.com	Yahoo!, Bing (Live), Alltheweb, Altavista, Ask, Gigablast, Entireweb, Wikipedia	Erases personal search information. International phone directory.
Jux2 www.jux2.com	Google, Yahoo! and Bing (MSN)	
Kartoo www.kartoo.com	"Uses the best search engines" (before: Yahoo!, Live, Ask, Exalead, Open Directory, Altavista, Alltheweb, etc.)	Graphic presentation. Possible to choose which search services Kartoo should use for searches. Anonymous search.
Mamma www.mamma.com	Yahoo!, Bing (Live), Ask (Ads by Google numbered in the hit lists!)	Video search. US Yellow Pages and White Pages.
MetaCrawler www.metacrawler.com	Google, Yahoo!, Bing (MSN), Ask, About (Ads by Google numbered in the hit lists!)	All four large search engines. Image-, sound- and video searches. US Yellow Pages and White Pages. Search tip-function: Are you looking for?
Surfwax www.surfwax.com	Alltheweb, Yahoo!, CNN News	Shows extracts from the hits.

5. Choosing Search Service

Searching on the Web?

Why information searching on the Web is popular:

- You do it yourself. You don't need to be entirely sure of what you're looking for, in contrast to when you have to ask someone who you don't know very well (e.g. a librarian).
- Easier to get going – you enter something and you almost always get a result.
- The sensation of uneasiness that characterizes the first phases of the information seeking process is rapidly reduced, since you have, in any case, found something.
- You get a feeling of knowing what you're doing. Your self-confidence increases as you have found certain things and thus don't need any help.
- You get the idea that you're dealing with a source, since you can, practically speaking, find just anything with the help of a search engine. Most of the time you don't need to understand how different databases function.
- It's fast and easily accessible (round the clock, the year around), also from mobile phones.

But there are also many emotional disadvantages: insecurity and hesitation, confusion, frustration and time pressure. The searching on the Net often takes more time than what you had imagined. The false roads are many. *Wilfing* is a new term for when you have gone astray and start thinking "what was I looking for?".

Another problem is "information overload"; you become flushed with information and can't handle it all. When a search results in a million hits you may perhaps give it up and look for an encyclopaedia instead. And how do you know when you're done with the search? When you have found enough or everything?

Much information is still not out on the Net but must be sought for in physical books and journals. Is the Net a possible information source for you?

Many different ways of searching lead to information on the Web, but some of the ways are efficient and others are less efficient. In the same way different search paths lead to different kinds of information. And different search methods lead to better or worse hits. Really inefficient searches lead to a lot of noise, i.e. lots of irrelevant information, or, if the worst comes to the worst, to no productive result at all.

Directory or search engine?

Directories and search engines are nearly each other's opposites. The seven points below illustrate important aspects of the search services.

	Directory	Search engine
Data collection	manual	automatic
Contents	qualitative	quantitative
Search method	in a hierarchic subject structure	using search words
Result	all links in the category	estimated relevance
Size	naturally small	unlimited
Size today (largest)	around 5 million (Open Directory)	more than 20 billion
Comparison with book	table of contents	register (index)

The data collection in a search engine takes place automatically by means of spiders, but in the directory an editor places the link. At the same time, the editor makes a quality selection, something which doesn't exist in the search engine.

The links in the directory are placed in a subject structure and found together with the other links in a given category. In the search engine you can't navigate a subject structure but have to look for relevant pages using search words which the search engine then ranks.

The directory doesn't have a maximum size, but is entirely dependent upon the editors having the time to add links at the same time as the already placed links need to be checked regularly. In the same manner, the search engine doesn't have any upper limit for its size, but here are limitations as well. The management of a large index requires more computer power, computers cost money and in the end it's all about finances. The idea is also for the seeker to quickly get the hit list once the search is done. A too large index can result in a too long wait and the seeker will then make a change of search service.

Should you use a search engine or a directory service? The answer is often both but below you find some guiding principles.

When should I use a search engine?
- When you have a small or obscure subject or concept that you need to search for.
- When you're looking for up-to-date information in a subject that you're familiar with.

- When you're looking for a specific Web site.
- When you want to search the entire text of millions of Web pages.
- When you want to get a large number of documents in your subject.
- When you're searching for a special type of document or a certain file type.
- When you want to search a certain Web site.
- When you want to use a newer search technique as, e.g., clustering of results or link analysis.

When should I use a directory?
- When you have a broad subject or concept that you're searching for.
- When you want a list of Web sites, of immediate interest to your subject. Sometimes the Web sites are also described or commented.
- When you're in the beginning of an investigation of a subject. Use a directory to find search words and phrases that can be used in other search services.
- When you don't know exactly what you're looking for but would recognize it when you see it.
- When you want to look around in a checked environment.
- When you'd rather get a few Web sites than lots of separate Web pages.
- When you want to avoid documents of small contents, which often show up in search engines.
- When you're searching for titles, links, comments or keywords to relevant material instead of the full-text material.

Below you find some examples of subjects and the suitable type of search service to start the search in. The subjects are commented after the table.

Directory	Search engine
Swedish literature	Astrid Lindgren
Second World War	the transit traffic through Sweden
Space journeys	Christer Fuglesang

Astrid Lindgren is the author of the books about Pippi Longstocking, Karlsson on the Roof, etc. *The transit traffic through Sweden*: During the Second World War German soldiers were transported on the Swedish railroad to Norway, which was occupied by Germany, in spite of the Swedish neutrality. *Christer Fuglesang* was the first Swedish person in space. He is a researcher and an ESA astronaut.

In short: General subjects in a directory and specific subjects in a search engine.

Assessing search services

Search services are extremely changeable. The technique is improved/changed, functions are added or disappear, services are bought by competitors and turned into shells for other search services (as Altavista has become to Yahoo!). Practically all search services suffer from bad documentation. Many features are not mentioned in the help texts and the texts are very general, particularly when it comes to ranking and sponsored links.

What should you look for when you assess a search service?
Test the search possibilities and the capacity of the service that you are about to use. Read the help- or tips page and skim over the FAQ (if there are any).

Search engines
- How many Web pages does the index contain?
- Are the bought/sponsored hits placed in the hit list or outside of it?
- Does the index contain many links that don't work (dead links)?
- What does the hit list look like?
- Are the hits relevant?
- How are the results presented?
- Are there sponsored links? How are they presented/marked out?
- What is the coverage? How large is the index?
- Where does the index come from?

Directories
- How many links does the directory contain (large or small)?
- Who is behind the directory (if it's not financed by advertising)?
- Does the directory include the search subject of interest to you?
- Is the directory maintained (dead links or old links)?

Meta search services
Which search services does the meta search service use for its searching?
- Search engines
- Directories
- Advertising services
- Other (e.g. Wikipedia)

What does the hit list look like?
- Are the hits relevant?
- How are the results presented?
- Are there sponsored links? How are they presented/marked out?
- From which search services do the hits come from?

What search possibilities exist?

- Which Boolean expressions support the service? (AND, OR, NOT, +, -)
- Can you truncate?
- Is phrase searching supported?
- Is field searching supported?
- Can the results be limited to a domain or a Web site?
- Can the results presentation be varied in any way?
- Is it possible to limit or revise the search?
- Is there any help for the search expression formulation (advanced searching in, e.g., Google is really a type of help, making the search syntax accessible)?

Comparing searches in different search engines

Thumbshots Ranking (http://ranking.thumbshots.com) is a service which compares the first hundred hits for different searches in some search engines. The following search engines can be compared in this service:

- Alltheweb (the Yahoo! index)
- Altavista (the Yahoo! index)
- Google
- MSN (Bing)
- Yahoo!

It's also possible to compare different search strings in the same search engine. The example below shows two searches in Google on the closely related terms *invisble web* and *deep web*.

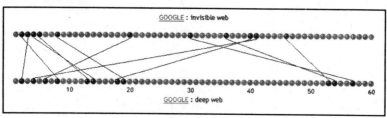

Fig. Comparison between "invisible web" and "deep web" in Google

The overlapping between the searches in the example is only 17 per cent and the differences between the placings in the hit lists (hit 1-60) are shown with the lines. See also comparisons in the chapter about search engines.

More things to consider when choosing a search service

Search limitations

Be clear on any possible limitations regarding time, language and geography. It matters for the choice of search service.

Specific query

If you have a specific, delimited query, use the search engines.

Circling around

A Web directory allows you to get a look at the subject and then make your delimitation.

6. The Search Process and the Search Query

The eight steps of the search process

The researcher Gary Marchionini[1] has produced a model of the information-seeking process for computer-based searches. The model consists of eight phases and the transitions between them are divided into three different types depending upon how common they are.

The phases:

1. Recognize and accept an information problem
2. Define and understand the problem
3. Choose a search system
4. Formulate a query
5. Execute search
6. Examine results
7. Extract information
8. Reflect/iterate/stop

The arrows in the model illustrate how complex the search process is. We constantly move from one phase to another when we seek information.

---

[1] Marchionini, Gary, *Information Seeking in Electronic Environments*, 1995.

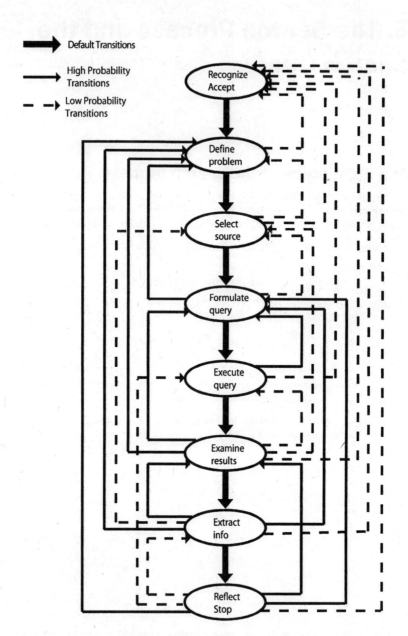

Fig. The search process for electronic information seeking according to Gary Marchionini.[2]

2 Marchionini, Gary, *Information Seeking in Electronic Environments*, 1995.

1. Recognize and accept an information problem

The process starts with the recognition and acceptance of an information need. In many cases we don't accept the information needs, i.e. we don't bother about searching for information in the subject since we don't find it worth the trouble.

2. Define and understand the problem

To narrow down a subject and formulate it as a problem (a sentence with a question mark at the end) is an important part of the search process which is easy to neglect. Once you have the problem formulation you also have a couple of search words to start out with. The problem formulation saves a lot of time and it's easy to go back and look at the problem formulation during the search to keep the search on the right track.

Besides formulating the search subject as a problem you should also try to answer the following questions as early as possible in the process:

* Which are the central aspects? Identify important concepts or keywords.
* What is the information meant for? Which is the level of ambition?
* Must the information be updated?
* How extensive does the information collection need to be?
* What previous knowledge do you have? Do you have to spend time on studying up on the subject?
* Which languages and geographical areas are of interest?
* Is scientific material required?
* How much time can the search take?

Be clear on any possible limitations in time, languages and geography. These limitations are also of importance to your choice of search service.

3. Choose a search system

Is the Internet the right place for searching, considering your subject? Is the sought information perhaps local or old? In that case the information is far from always on the Net. Is the information completely new? If so, it might not yet be published, or it may be hard to find in the traditional search services.

Would it be faster to find the information in another way? Pure facts can be easy to find in ordinary encyclopaedias. You often spend more time and energy on searches than you would have if you had visited the nearest library. Learn what you may expect to find on the Net and what normally won't show up.

The type of search that you are about to perform matters to your choice of search service. For an exhaustive search, where "all" information in the subject is the goal, many search services must be used. No individual search engine or directory covers more than one part of the Web and all of them hold unique resources.

If you want to get an overview of the central resources in a subject you should use the large Web directories. These "virtual collections" provide a very good starting point when you begin looking for information in a broad subject.

If you have a specific, delimited query you should use the search engines. For the monitoring of new resources in a subject you can use different news services or *alerts* in a search engine.

Before you choose your search service you should do some thinking about the subject and what you're trying to find. Never rely on only one service or Web site.

4. Formulate a query

The possibility of getting good search results increases the more you prepare your search query. To do a search with just words, without conditioning the search, will often give hit quantities with the relevant hits mixed with so much garbage that you will be giving up before having gone through just a fraction of the hits.

Formulate the search query as clearly as possible. Sort it into interesting and uninteresting aspects.

Analyse the search query. Pick out central keywords and phrases. Look up synonyms, alternative spellings, abbreviations and acronyms which you can use in the search.

Use articles, books and other resources that you know about in order to find new search words.

5. Execute search

The phase can be described as "the interaction with one or several information systems". In practice this means that you enter the search query in Google and push the search button, you call the admittedly knowledgeable professor or you look in the books in a library.

6. Examine results

Is the query answered or the goal fulfilled? If not, what remains and how will you get there? Perhaps the search needs to be modified or the goal/query revalued. This may lead to a change of search strategy:

- Broaden the search?
- Narrow the search?
- Change search service?
- Look for another type of material?
- Go off-line? Go to the library's physical collections or contact a specialist in the subject?

7. Extract information

To extract information is the goal of the search process. The collecting on the Web is often done "on the go"; you pick up some here and some there. When it comes to searches in databases the collecting is done much more systematically, perhaps by means of your library.

8. Reflect/iterate/stop

Is the search done and the information need met with? What lessons can be learned before the next search? Sometimes you have to start from the beginning, i.e. redefine and reformulate the problem.

Modes of action, strategies and tactics

On the Net and in books and articles on information seeking you'll find many terms for different ways of executing a search. The most common denomination is *strategies* (variants are *search strategies* or *information seeking strategies*), but *tactics* are also used at times. It may be good to bear this in mind if you want to read more about the subject.

The information need and the search query

An information need can look many different ways. Perhaps you need to get an overview of a certain subject or perhaps you only have to check a fact. Having to update yourself in a subject can also create an information need, just as a need of specialization will.

Irrespective of if you are preparing a major purchase, e.g. of a car, or if you have an assignment for school, you often need more information and you are forced to search for information. Each information need requires a certain type of information. And different kinds of information require different modes of procedure.

The standard procedure for clarifying an information need is to try to write it down as a question. When the question is formulated it's normally possible to refine and distil its components. Well formulated questions can more often be answered than less well formulated questions.

By reading up on a subject, e.g. in an encyclopaedia, you can often find central aspects, useful terms and words to search on.

Query types

Search queries that correspond to information needs can be divided in different ways. A basic division is constituted by self-limiting respective open search queries. The self-limiting queries have a specific answer, and in most cases you'll know, during the course of the information seeking process, whether you have found the answer or not. Open queries, however, can't be said to have an answer, but are answered with *sufficient* information.

Five query types, of falling magnitude, when it comes to scope[3]:

Overview

What is there to be found in a specific subject/what types of resources exist? Example: Different types of resources about alcohol. Resources that deal with alcohol: kinds, sales, drinks, harmfulness...

General information

Queries on general information/broad subjects. Example: Resources that deal with the Middle Ages.

Delimit/expand the query

The transition between general and specific queries, i.e. queries that deal with the delimitation or expansion of a subject.

Specific information

Queries on specific information in well-defined areas. Example: Information about the National Gallery in Prague.

Facts

Pure fact queries with a given answer. Example: What is the name of the mayor in New York City?

Catch the query

By putting your question into words, by formulating it, you're forced to think about what you want. If you spend time identifying key phrases and visualizing the ideal answer you will have a much greater chance of recognizing that answer once you find it on the Web.

The question can perhaps not always be "caught", but can often be narrowed down through considering the following before the search: Who? What? When? Where? Why? How?

Who?

Who's important in your subject? There may be a known expert or organization that you should contact. Do you need to find someone with certain experience or knowledge? Think in several steps: Who knows the person who might be able to help you? Good places to start searching for organizations are directories or link collections. Experts can often be found through media resources like newspaper archives.

---

[3] The division comes from Johanna Nilsson's Master's Thesis *Informationssökning på Internet - att välja verktyg* [Information seeking on the Internet—choosing tools] (1998).

What?

What kind of information do you need? Information comes in many shapes: statistics, first-hand sources from an event, background information, specific facts or scientific articles. What would be the best source of information? What is the information meant for? Different kinds of information are needed for different purposes, like an analysis or a report, an overview of a subject or a confirmation of some factual information. By defining the genre of the information sought after it will be easier to choose search service and to pick the right search words.

When?

When did the researched event take place? If you're not dealing with a contemporary event you have to find sources that go back in time sufficiently. Databases hidden in the Deep Web or old web pages in the Old Web can be useful resources (Chapter 11).

Where?

Where did the researched event take place or from where did the researched person come? There is often more information locally about events or persons. Consider whether a geographical delimitation might be of interest.

Where may the question have been asked earlier? There are few subjects that have never been discussed earlier; there may be relevant information in newspapers, TV broadcasts, court documents, Web discussions and so on. Make use of what others have done earlier, don't do all the research work from scratch if you can avoid it. Where are you likely to find the largest, most suitable collection of information? Large quantities of information can be found, e.g., in university libraries, in subject databases and in the daily papers and other media companies.

Why?

Why do you need to do the research? The reason may be everything from finding someone to interview or confirm certain facts to getting the hang of a big subject or completing a school assignment. Why? is often close related to What?, the purpose often defines what information you need to search for.

How?

How much information do you need? The need may stretch from a separate fact to everything that a subject comprises. The information need may determine what kind of search service to use, e.g. a search engine or some kind of a directory.

How will you use the information? Different requirements are placed on information that is to be used printed (newspaper or book) compared to a wedding speech. And how up-to-date does the information need to be? The degree of newness determines the way of searching. Topical information may be hard to find in the search engines. Old information can be hard to find in electronic forms, but check the Old Web.

Formulate the search query

To formulate the search query in a search engine you can follow the steps below. The point is to define exactly what you're looking for, the ideal Web page, and then design the search based on this ideal. The search query should reach the relevant Web pages for your subject, at the same time as pages not needed should be excluded.

1. Imagine the ideal Web page with all the information that you need.

Example: You're looking for information about the Swedish author Jan Arnald who is one of the editors of the Swedish literature journal Aiolos. The ideal Web page would contain Jan Arnald's entire biography, preferably with photographs.

2. Think of the words that would be on your ideal Web page.

Example: The ideal Web page would contain both the word Arnald and the word Aiolos. With Boolean logic the search query will be:

aiolos AND arnald

But since AND is preselected in the large search engines it is enough to enter:

aiolos arnald

3. Think of an exact phrase that exists on your ideal Web page, two or more words that follow upon each other.

Example: Instead of just searching on the surname you can search on the whole name as a phrase:

"jan arnald"

4. Think of the words that you don't want to form part of the search, words that lead to pages which are not of any use to you.

Example: Jan Arnald has also written detective stories under the pseudonym Arne Dahl and as he is better known as a detective-story writer many of the pages will probably be about the detective stories, and not about the literature journal Aiolos that you were interested in. Therefore we will exclude Arne Dahl from the search by means of NOT in the Boolean logic. In the search engines NOT is represented by a minus sign (-) before the word or phrase that is to be excluded:

-"arne dahl"

5. Run the query.

Example: Enter the search query in the search engine and execute the search.

aiolos "jan arnald" -"arne dahl"

6. *Improve the search.*

In a typical search on the Net in a search engine you have to try over and over again. You will be improving the searching constantly as you learn more and more about the subject. New, more efficient search words are discovered and more aspects to remove from the search will be thought of.

Different types of search queries

There is not always a cut-and-clear information need behind search queries; they can instead be divided into three categories:[4]

- ◆ **Information** – the intention is to find information.
- ◆ **Navigation** – the intention is to find a specific Web site for searching/surfing.
- ◆ **Transaction** – the intention is to perform an activity on a Web site, e.g. Net shopping or look in a library directory.

Search tips

Clear and unclear queries
Use directories for large queries, or when the query is unclear. And use search engines when you have a clear idea of what you're looking for and when you have good search words, ready for use.

The formulation of the search query
Formulate the search query as clearly as possible. Sort it into interesting and uninteresting aspects.

Analyze the search query
Pick out central keywords and phrases. Find synonyms, alternative spellings, abbreviations and acronyms that you can use in the search.

Revalue the goal of your search
One search query is not enough even to very experienced Web searchers. One or two modifications are often required. And good searchers often revalue the goal of the search after the first search.

Alternative way
On the Web there are often several ways to reach the imagined destination. If it's impossible to get ahead on the planned route you have to find another way to reach the goal.

---

[4] Broder, Andrei (2002) A taxonomy of web search [http://www.sigir.org/forum/F2002/broder.pdf].

Track Web pages

Use search engines to get back to pages earlier visited. By remembering fragments of the page, which provides you with search words, it's often easy to track the page.

Execute the search using several services parallelly

Through using several search services at the same time you can, in an easy manner, make use of the information that you've found in a service to get on with your search. Use the retrieved information in the next service in order to find more relevant information.

Cut and paste

"Cut and paste" makes information seeking with computers more efficient than searches in old card catalogues and large bibliographies (books about books).

The Net dealers

Use the online stores, like amazon.com. They contain large quantities of information. They also often contain tips about similar products or services and comments from other users.

Find new search words

Use articles, books and other resources that you know of to find new search words.

Self-publishing

The Net is a medium for self-publishing. Anybody can publish practically anything. Everything found on the Net needs to be examined and analyzed before it can be used.

Not just Google

Don't use only Google. Google is fantastic, but there are lots of other useful services. Through other services you can find information which won't show up in Google's hit lists.

Different search routes

The three most important routes to information on the Web are the search engines, the Web directories and awareness about the Deep/Invisible Web. They are useful for different types of search queries, so make sure that you understand the differences.

7. Search Strategies

Different types of information seeking

There are many types of information seeking. It could concern:

+ Hunting for specific information, perhaps a single fact.
+ Collecting of information to be forwarded, i.e., sending it on to somebody else.
+ Tracing information for retrieval, i.e., a search for a known object, perhaps a Web page that you have visited earlier.
+ Collecting of information for later reading and processing.
+ Browsing information for learning, i.e., surfing around on subject Web sites or looking through these in a specific subject.
+ Making an exhaustive search, i.e., getting all the information about a subject.

The mode of procedure when searching for factual information is not the same as when you collect information for later processing. Certain general modes of procedure exist. You always have two different ways to go about your search:

+ Do a broad search and then narrow it down little by little.
+ Do a narrow search and broaden it if required.

Broad searching may mean that you're using few or general search words when you execute the search. Then you add more words or substitute general words for more specific words.

Narrow searching means to start out from several narrow and specific search words in the search. Then you remove words or you substitute specific words for general words.

Searching versus browsing

When searching on the Web there are two fundamentally different ways of searching. The first one is to follow links, i.e., to click yourself forward in your hunt for information. To follow links is often called surfing or browsing, depending upon how conscious the clicking is. Surfing is more random and unfocused than the browsing which is conscious and controlled.

The other way of searching is to search with words in a search service or within a Web site. Word searches are sometimes called analytical searching as it requires you to analyze your search subject and choose search words before you begin to search. When it comes to browsing you don't have to have the search query formulated or chosen your search words, but can narrow down the sought information gradually.

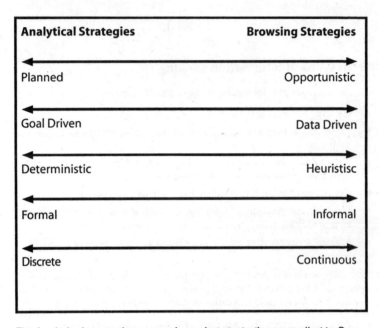

Fig. Analytical strategies versus browsing strategies according to Gary Marchionini.[1]

As the figure above illustrates, analytical strategies and browsing strategies differ in many different ways. The employment of the different search modes often depend upon the system in which you're doing your search and what you're searching for. We are no doubt also different as individuals and probably prefer different ways of searching.

Analytical strategies

The Booelan operators (AND and OR) occur in some part of the strategies below, they are further explained in Chapter 8.

1Marchionini, Gary, *Information Seeking in Electronic Environments*, 1995.

Building blocks

The different concepts of the search query form search strings that are then combined. Traditionally, in databases one search has been executed for each block before combining them to a final search.

Example

Search query: I want to find information about medical libraries or hospital libraries in the Swedish neighbouring cities Lund or Malmö.

The blocks might then look like this:

Block 1: *lund OR malmö*
Block 2: *hospital library OR (hospital AND library)*
Block 3: *"medical library"*

In the final search the blocks are combined to a complete search string and a parenthesis is used for a correct combination of the blocks:

Final search: *(lund OR malmö) AND (hospital library OR [hospital AND library] OR "medical library")*

Facet searching

If a search consists of two or various separate terms the different parts are called facets. Within each facet the search words may be supplemented with synonyms and other closely related terms. Everything to get as good coverage as possible for the facet. The different facets are then combined in a joint search.

Example

If you're looking for information about transport costs the facets will be *transport* and *costs*. The transport facet can be increased by *freight* and *"shipment of goods"* (one phrase, must be marked with quotation marks). The terms should be combined with OR so that only one of the search words is required to get a hit. Costs can in the other facet be supplemented with *price*. The two facets are combined with AND. The search string will be:

(transport OR freight OR "shipment of goods") AND (cost OR costs OR price)

A variant of the facet search is "successive fractions". This means that the original, big search block is narrowed down little by little with increasingly finer limitations by adding more narrow concepts.

You can also start with the most specific concept. In that way you can work more efficiently by not having to do part of the work with fractions as you start out with a smaller amount.

Pearl growing

Pearl growing means that you pull out search words from a relevant document, e.g., through citing a name or subject word. Through the search concepts that have been fished out (the pearls) new documents are found that have a connection with the first one (more pearls).

If you have a good reference to start out from, e.g., a good Web page, you can grow this information. In a search engine you can often do a search with the operator *link:* to get the Web pages that have linked to the page of interest. The Web pages that have linked to your resource page may contain relevant information or link to other similar pages.

Example

Internetbrus.com is a Swedish Web blog about searching and search services on the Internet. In Google you can search for the pages that link to this very page by writing

link:Internetbrus.com

In Google you shouldn't enter http://, but www should be entered if the address includes this.

You can do the same with books in a Net bookstore. If you find your book you can often see what other books customers of your chosen book have bought; you might get lucky. In Amazon (www.amazon.com), for example, you can also search on the categories that the book belongs to.

Interactive scanning

Interactive scanning means that you search through a great number of relevant documents for key concepts to formulate new problems, which may then result in new search queries.

Simple searching (quick-and-dirty)

A simple search is a search on one or a couple of search words combined with AND or OR. No subtleties are used and the result, in any case in databases, will be rough but it will provide a first image. Sometimes the term *quick-and-dirty* is used by "pro searchers" for simple searches as the very art of searching just because it's fast, but the result is a bit messy. Almost all searches on the Web are simple searches.

Browsing strategies

The browsing strategies are important ways to search the Web as they can make use of the Web's nature of using links. Traditionally, browsing hasn't been considered as professional as analytical searching, in part owing to the connections that the companies in the search business have with the database industry. Perhaps it's not until now, with the Web and the new generation of services sometimes called Web 2.0, that browsing may be seen as equal in merit to analytical searching.

Specific browsing

Specific (controlled) browsing is systematic, focused on a specific object or goal, e.g., the scanning of a list of known objects to verify facts.

Predictive browsing

Predictive (semi-controlled) browsing is generally purposeful, the goal is less delimited or clear and the browsing is less systematic.

General browsing

General (uncontrolled) browsing doesn't have a real goal and very little focus, e.g., flipping through a magazine and zapping the TV.

Berrypicking

Berrypicking is, broadly speaking, a browsing strategy, but with elements of analytical searching. It's really a searching behaviour which most of us have and that has been formalized and named. Berrypicking means to collect, or pick, information little by little as you find it, like other browsing, but you actually do it irrespective of search system or search strategy. The search is done in the same way as berry picking in the woods, unplanned but still structured and adapted to the surroundings.[2]

Other search strategies

Besides searching with words or browsing there are a few other ways to search:

Enter the URL

To enter a Web address requires previous knowledge of the address or an idea of where the sought information may be found. If you know that all Swedish municipalities have URLs set up according to the same pattern (www.nameofmuniciaplity.se) it's not so hard to figure out that Ronneby municipality is found at www.ronneby.se and Stockholm municipality at www.stockholm.se. Likewise you may

---

2 Bates, Marcia J. "The Design of Browsing and Berrypicking Techniques for the Online Search Interface." *Online Review* 13 (October 1989): 407-424. [http://www.gseis.ucla.edu/faculty/bates/berrypicking.html]

conclude that there will be quite a bit of information about space at www.nasa.
gov.

Monitoring a subject

If you have a constant interest in a subject there are several ways to monitor what's
going on. Different variants are:

- ♦ Standing search in a search engine (*alert*) – you receive a mail when
  there are new matches for your search terms.

- ♦ E-mail lists – through membership in an e-mail list information about
  the list theme is sent to your inbox. Companies or interest groups may
  have newsletters and in this way you'll be getting new information. Or
  the list may be intended for like-minded people who can send letters
  (and reply) to the list.

Two-step searching

Two-step searching is an indirect search, e.g., to rapidly find sought information or
to find information which can't be found through the search engines. The search
is done in various steps (at least two). You have to do the search in two steps, first
find the place which holds the information and then look in that place. As far as
databases are concerned, the search page is often indexed in the search engines
and can thereby be found.

Three different two-step searches as examples:

- ♦ Middle Ages links: *site:www.museumof london.org.uk middle ages
  links* (in Google or other search engine depending on how site site: is
  handled).

- ♦ Databases about airplane crashes : *database "plane crash"* (in a search
  engine).

- ♦ Music by Apoptygma Berzerk for listening: *listen "apoptygma berzerk"*
  (in search engine).

Two-step searching is the most important search strategy on the Invisible Web,
see Chapter 11.

Search tips

Subject-specific words – *lingo*
For each search there is a vocabulary, a slang word or other unique words that
make it easier to get relevant hits.

Other interested parties

For most subjects there are at least a few interested people, and some of them have already put up a Web site, a forum or other resources on the Net in the subject where they collect and comment on relevant links. You can facilitate your search a lot by using these special resources instead of trying to build your own.

From the inside and out

When you search it's better to start with a very specific search query and then get increasingly more general. If you start with more general queries you will be flooded with hits. If the search doesn't work, make it slowly more general until you find a good balance between the number of hits and the contents of the hits. – More is not better!

A loved child has many names

Most things, unfortunatly, have nicknames. New York can be NY, Carl-Gustav can be CG or Calle. Nicknames have to be included in an exhaustive search.

Just the right puzzle piece

You never know which piece of information will be the one which brings your entire search together. So keep your eyes open, look for each fragment of information that has the potential to make your search complete.

Don't forget your fellow human being

When you're searching on the Net it's important to remember that there is a world beyond the Internet. Web pages are created by human beings and sometimes human beings are the most important resource you can find.

Constant change

The Web is constantly expanding, constantly changing, constantly breaking down (unfortunately), and constantly rebuilt. If you're planning to do continuing investigations it's important to have a strategy to keep informed about all the new Web sites and resources in your subject. (See Chapters 12 and 15)

Increase your search power

If you use the Web site's special syntax you'll increase the power in your searches considerably. If you mix the special syntaxes you'll increase the power in your searches still more. But be careful. (See Chapter 8)

Be critical

You should take each page on the Internet with a grain of salt. (See Chapter 9)

Many roads lead to the same place

On the Web there are often several ways to reach the intended destination. If it's impossible to get ahead on the route you planned, you have to find another way to reach your goal.

Stored knowledge

The speed and range of the Internet is awfully seductive, but remember that most of humanity's saved knowledge is stored in non-electronic, durable media. Written or printed text is the biggest source, but information may also be extracted from sculptures, monuments and other cultural objects.

Go directly to the source

If possible, you should go directly to the source. If there are authorities, institutions or organizations connected to the subject area you're interested in, you'll probably find links on their Web sites. Many of these have librarians or Web editors who work professionally with information in the area.

8. Search Technique

Select search words

Good and bad search words

When you use search engines the distillation of good search words often constitutes the key to a successful search. Words that describe important parts of the query.

Good search words are unique or uncommon. Common words generate large number of hits, but can be added to other words in a search query to get the right angle of the more uncommon words.

All words should be correctly spelled. But if you have trouble with the spelling just relax, the major search engines suggest spelling alternatives. If there are different spellings of a word, try to search on each word in Google or some other search engine to see which version of the word generates most hits and then use that spelling. Or use both variants in your search strategy. Misspelt words only generate hits which are also misspelt.

Bad search words are ambiguous words, words with several meanings like break or light. But like common words they are useful as search words in combination with other words. The words define the context of each other. For example light together with sun is completely different from light together with calories.

Small, common words like and aren't always indexed by the search engines because they are too common. These words are called stop words and are often excluded from the search when entered in a search engine. But stop words can be used in phrases, so the stop words are often indexed in some way.

Describe the question/query with synonyms and with more concepts. This won't limit the query, it will just focus it.

The best words first

Place the best words first when you do a search in a search engine. In certain search services the first terms are given more consideration. And place related words next to each other, sometimes this will affect the relevance estimation. At times it may pay off to change the word order in the search query.

Think like a Web page

Don't select search words that represent your subject – instead select the search words that you think will show up on the pages that are relevant to your search.

Assess and do a new search

Assess the search string quickly. If no. 1-10 in the hit list aren't relevant, then why should no. 25 be relevant? Change the search words and do a new search instead of looking over all the first 30 hits.

Remove undesired aspects

If a search word has several meanings and the search result is imprecise you can remove undesired aspects. On the search engines' pages for advanced searches you can often select "without these words" or something similar, which means that the word may not occur on the pages in the hit list. Alternatively you can enter a minus sign before the search word in the usual search box, e.g., -saab.

Search word suggestions

Yahoo! gives suggestions for searches when you start writing words into the search box. This is a good help to define searches in real time. The Web browser Firefox's search box also provides search word suggestions.

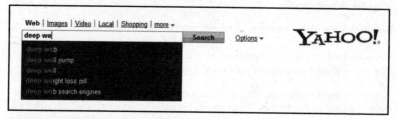

Fig. Yahoo! gives search word suggestions.

Phrase searching

A phrase is a group of words that have to stand next to each other in a certain order. Most search engines use quotation marks (" ") to mark a phrase, e.g., "the invisible web". It is used to specify a search.

Phrase searching is particularly important in languages where words are not compound words. Compare *information seeking behaviour* with the Swedish *informationssökningsbeteende* (the three words have become one compound word).

Be careful with searching on phrases. Phrase searching may be a good way to define searches but should only be used for words that normally appear next to each other, e.g., "association of information specialists" (name of an association). Even proper names may be problematic. A search on *"george bush"* would miss references to George W Bush.

Simple and advanced searching

Most search engines and databases have something that they call simple searching on their start page. You fill in your search words in a search box. You can also enter the search service's special syntax in the search box, commands which specify and define. But you reach most of the special functions of the search services easier by searching on the page for advanced searching. The simple searching has its advantages and is efficient when you know what you're looking for, e.g., a specific Web site.

Almost all search engines and databases have a form containing more choices than the simple search. It may be called advanced searching, expert searching or enhanced searching. But you don't need to be an expert to use the advanced search, on the contrary. In the advanced search many of the search service's possibilities are often split up in a simple manner. In this way you often get clues to how you can improve your search.

On the search engines' pages for advanced searching there are often forms for searches with Boolean logic (described in the next section). Google's page is shown below, but the pages of the other search engines are rather similar.

Fig. Page for advanced search in Google.

On Google's page under the heading "Find Web pages that have..." you get possibilities:

- With all these words – an AND-search, AND is placed between the words that are entered here.
- With the exact phrase – the words that are entered are handled as a phrase, quotation marks are not needed.
- With one or more of these words – an OR-search, OR is placed between the entered words.
- Under that there is yet another possibility, "But don't show pages that have... any of these unwanted words" – a NOT-search, the word which is entered is not found among the hits.

The search possibilities are easy to combine, but be careful. If all the possibilities are used it's easy to do very specific searches, perhaps so specific that the hit list will only consist of a single hit.

Boolean logic

The Internet can be seen as a big database and searches for content must, therefore, follow the rules for computer-based data mining. Computers work with ones and zeros, yes and no. When searching with Boolean logic you set up conditions that have to be met in the search. All search engines use Boolean logic in the search query formulation, but in somewhat different ways. Make sure that you understand the different operators: AND, OR and NOT.

Search engines generally have a preset Boolean operator. This means that the space between the entered search words either means OR or AND. Nowadays it's normally AND that is preset, but look in the help texts to be on the safe side. In the infancy of the search engines OR was common as the preselection in order for the searcher to get more hits.

There are three basic operators in Boolean logic: AND, OR and NOT. They are often written in English. By means of the operators the search words are combined to execute more specific searches.

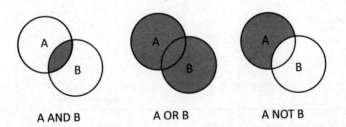

A AND B   A OR B   A NOT B

Fig. The three Boolean operators

In the figure above the darker fields represent that which is retrieved through the different searches.

AND

A AND B

Search query: I'm interested in the relationship between work and stress.

An AND-search requires that both (all if several) search words are retrieved in the document for it to be on the hit list.

A AND B – When using AND the hit must contain both word A and word B.

Example in Google:

work: 1.56 billion hits
stress: 169 million hits
work AND stress: 40.5 million hits

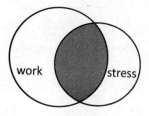

The more words you combine in an AND-search, the fewer documents are retrieved, as each of the documents has to contain all of the search words. By adding yet another word in the AND-search the search is further defined.

work AND stress AND "sick leave": 70 500 hits

OR

A OR B – When using OR the hit must contain at least one of the words A and B.

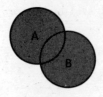

A OR B

Search query: I want information about universities and university colleges.

In Sweden both university college and university are used as terms for higher education. The search needs to result in hits for at least one of the concepts and therefore OR is used.

Example in Yahoo!
"corvus frugilegus" (rook) 241 000 hits
"corvus corone" (crow) 374 000 hits
"corvus frugilegus" OR *"corvus corone"* 451 000 hits

A search on *corvus frugilegus OR corvus corone* gives hits containing corvus frugilegus or corvus corone. The overlap of the two circles represents the documents that contain both terms (and which are retrieved in the AND-search).

OR is primarily used for synonyms or similar concepts. The more words used in an OR-search, the more hits are retrieved. The search becomes broader.

NOT

A NOT B – When using NOT the hit must contain the word A but not the word B.

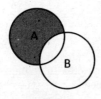

A NOT B

Search query: I want information about dogs, but nothing about cats.

Only documents where dog occurs, but not cat, are retrieved. If both dog and cat occur, the document won't be part of the hit list. You should therefore be careful with this type of searches; important documents or central resources may easily be excluded.

Example in Google
cat 678 million
dog 300 million
cat NOT dog, i.e. *cat -dog* (see below) 576 million

The search above gives hits which contain dog but which don't contain cat.

Combine the operators

The operators can be used together with phrase searching and parentheses. An example:

(university OR "university college") AND uk NOT london

The search string gives hits containing *university* or *university college* together with *uk*. No hit contains *london*. Relevant material may of course be screened out because it contains the word london, but if we're dealing with a large amount of hits this might not matter. The parentheses determine in which order the expressions will be searched. The operators first work within a parenthesis, and thereafter with the whole expression (or the next parenthesis if there are more).

Boolean logic in practice

There are several different ways to use the Boolean operators when searching the Internet. In a search engine the operators can be used in three ways, but all search engines don't support all types of uses.

- ♦ Full Boolean logic with the operators.
- ♦ Applied Boolean logic at searches (simple searching).
- ♦ Predetermined search language in a form (advanced searching).

Full Boolean logic with the operators

In many search engines you can search by means of the logical operators, e.g.,

feline AND food AND senior

See Boolean logic earlier in this chapter for more examples.

Applied Boolean logic at simple searching

When you do a simple search with several words in the search engine's simple search box it's often an AND-search that is done. In the infancy of the search engines (and the Web) OR was preselected to increase the number of hits. Today AND is preselected in all big search engines to give better precision and to avoid a flooding of hits.

You can normally use + (plus) and - (minus) in the simple searching. + works like an AND and can secure the inclusion of so-called stop words, words which the search engine otherwise will exclude. To write + before each word is normally not necessary as AND is the preselected operator between the words. – is used as NOT, i.e., to exclude words from the search. E.g.:

lund -university

If you want to use OR you have to use the full Boolean logic or the form in the form for advanced searching.

Predetermined search langague in forms

Many search engines have a page called "advanced searching" or something similar. The page is often not particularly advanced, but offers the Boolean logic together with other search restrictions in a simple manner. The operators are generally described in common language. Examples from different search engines follow below:

AND
find pages with ALL these words
show results with ALL these words

OR
find pages with ANY of these words
show results with ANY of these words

NOT
find pages WITHOUT these words
show results with NONE of these words

Bing doesn't have a general page for "advanced searching." When you have done your search and got the hit list you can select "alternative" or "advanced" for search restrictions.

The search words – constants or variables?

The selected search words can be seen as constants or variables in the search depending upon which Boolean operator you place before the search word. AND and NOT make the search word function as a constant; the word needs to be present respective can't be present. OR, however, makes the search into a variable; the word or its alternative has to be present but not both of them.

Field searching

Most Web pages consist of more than just text. (See the introduction for basic HTML) These different parts, which are called fields, are searchable. In a search engine it can look like this:

♦ *domain:lu.se*
♦ *title:"information seeking"* (words in the title tag of the page)
♦ *link:www.lu.se* (the pages that link to www.lu.se)

◆ *inurl:guide* (the word must be in the URL)

Field searching is an important way of limiting a search in a search engine with millions of documents. Example: *title:"middle ages"* (in Google *intitle:"middle ages"*) gives more relevant hits than a search on just the Middle Ages. But many relevant pages will be missed as far from all pages about the Middle Ages have the Middle Ages in their titles.

Search in the Web address

Search in the URL to delimit the search. In the search engines you can normally search on the words in the URL (the Web address) as great parts of the URL are (may be) meaningful.

The anatomy of a URL:

http://en.wikipedia.org/wiki/Middle_Ages

1. protocol: http
2. name of Web server: en (often www)
3. domain name: wikipedia
4. top domain name: org
5. directory name: wiki
6. file name: Middle_Ages

Particularly the two last ones, the directory name and the file name, often contain subject words. But it's also worthwhile to search on the domain name, for example if you're looking for an organization or a brand.

Example: *url:"middle ages"/inurl:"middle ages"*gives pages that contain the words Middle Ages somewhere in the Web address.

Web site search

To find a page within a Web site or domain you can search with the delimitation *site:*. You'll then be searching on the domain name or top domain name, e.g., bbc.co.uk or volvo.com. In order to find information about Sweden at BBC's Web, search on sweden site: bbc.co.uk, which limits the search after sweden to bbc.co.uk.. When it comes to smaller top domains it might be useful to limit the search to a certain top domain, e.g., .se or .mil, but the big .com and .edu might be too big for the delimitation to be efficient, unless it's combined with several other search words.

Example in Google:

A search on the Swedish word for sugar (socker) in Google gives about 2 million hits. But if you limit the search to the Swedish National Food Administration (you add site:slv.se) the search will only give about 400 hits. If you do a search on the same word (socker) in the search engine at the Web site of the National Food Administration you get about 300 hits, i.e., a hundred fewer than in Google.

Site: works in among others Google, Yahoo! and Bing.

More search techniques

Proximity operators

If possible, use proximity operators, e.g., NEAR, instead of an AND between your search words to specify their connection. This guarantees that the words are found near each other in the document. Google automatically considers the proximity between the search words in the relevance calculation that is done to compile the hit list, but there is no possibility of specifying a distance between the words.

Always use at least two search words in your search

A search with two or three search words gives a much better result than a search with one word. A search on one word will almost always be too broad and a lot of noise will form part of the hit list. Each word that you add specifies the earlier ones. Example in Google:

phone gives 1.2 billion hits
phone number gives 128 million hits
phone number catalog gives 4.2 million hits
phone number catalog search gives 314 000 hits

The result is often considerably restricted by each added search word. In the example above over 90 per cent of the hits disappeared for each added search word.

Find other file types

If you search for special file types you have two alternatives. You can either use a search engine that is specialized on that particular file type, or you can search in a regular search engine. In a regular search engine you can restrict the search to only one file type. On the advanced search page there are often possibilities to choose the file type in a simple manner. But it means that the search engine must have the file type indexed for it to be found. When you search on the file extension, links to files of the desired type will also be part of the hit list, as a link to the file from the Web page is enough for inclusion.

An example of the usefulness of "similar pages" in Google

I was searching for a record that I had owned several years ago, a reggae collection with early ska and rocksteady. The record was released by a classic company, don't remember which one, and was the first in a series. Thought of a likely record company: Trojan Records. Checked their Web site but no luck. Not at Amazon music under reggae, ska or rocksteady either. Came to think of the Google function of "similar pages". Entered the Trojan Records URL in Google and searched. When Trojan Records came up in the hit list I chose "similar pages". And hey, first in the hit list was "Soul Jazz Records", which sounded familiar. At the Soul Jazz Records Web sites I found the record I was looking for – 100 % Dynamite.

Quick guide to Google

Basic examples	Finds pages which contain...
travel train	words travel and train
cambridge OR oxford	Either the word cambridge or the word oxford (or both words)
"we are the world"	the exact phrase we are the world
spider –search engine	the word spider but not the word search engine
google ~guide	the word google and the word guide with their synonyms, e.g. tips and help
define:firewall	definitions of the word firewall from the Web
"george * bush"	The words george and bush separated by exactly one word (gives, e.g., George W Bush or George Walker Bush)

Calculator	Means	Enter into the search box
+	addition	13 + 8
-	subtraction	21 - 8
*	multiplication	13 * 8
/	division	8 / 3
% of	per cent of	75% of 755
^ or **	raised to	2^6 or 2**6
old units in new units	convert units	30 euros in SEK or 30 feet in m

Restrict the search	Means	Enter into the search box (and result)
site:	Only searches within one Web site or domain.	*linux site:www.kth.se* (searches for linux at KTH, KTH is the Swedish abbreviation for the Royal Institute of Technology.) *linux site:.se* (searches for linux in the se-domain)
File type: (or ext:)	Only searches among indicated file type.	*population statistics file type:pdf* (PDF files with the phrase population statistics)
safesearch:	Excludes adult material.	*safesearch: sex* (searches for sex without presenting e.g. porn)

Alternative query types	Means	Enter into the search box (and result)
cache:	Shows Google's saved version of the Web page.	*cache:www.kb.se* (shows Google's saved version of the National Library of Sweden's first page)
info:	Shows info about the Web page.	*info:www.volvo.com* (shows the link's hit list text and several choices, among others cache: and related:
link:	Finds linked pages, i.e., pages which link to the URL.	*link:www.interpol.int* (pages which link to www.interpol.int)
related:	Lists Web pages which are similar or related to the URL.	*related:www.fbi.gov* (lists Web pages which are similar or relate to the FBI Web page)

Restrictions	Means	Enter into the search box (and result)
allinanchor:	All search words must be in the link text on the page.	*Allinanchor:invisible web* (pages which have links with *invisible web* in the link text)
inanchor:	The search word after inanchor: must be in a link text.	*used cars inanchor:cheap* (pages with the words *used cars* in the text and *cheap* in the link text)
allintext:	All search words must be in the text on the page.	*allintext: recipet banana curry chicken* (pages where the text contains the words *recipe, banana, curry* and *chicken*)

intext:	The search word after intext: must be in the text on the page.	*brightplanet intext:"deep web"* (pages with the word *brightplanet* and with the phrase *deep web* in the text)
allintitle:	All search words must be in the title of the page.	*allintitle:deep web* (pages that have the words *deep* and *web* in the title)
intitle:	The search word after intitle: must be in the title of the page.	*film cinema intitle:top list* (pages with the words *film* and *cinema* and with *top list* in the title)
allinurl:	All search words must be in the URL of the page.	*allinurl:google faq* (pages with the words *google* and *faq* in the URL)
inurl:	The search word after inurl: must be in the URL of the page.	*Information seeking inurl:guide* (pages with the phrase *information seeking* and with *guide* in the URL)

9. Assessment and Source Criticism

Several problems present themselves when searching on the Net. One that is becoming increasingly bigger is *information overload*; you become overloaded with information and perhaps you feel more like giving up than to start unraveling the information. Another problem is that the Web in many ways is a lawless country – anyone can publish just about anything. The differences are big compared to the books in a library which have normally undergone various examinations: the publishing editor, the fact editor and finally the librarian who buys them. Not for nothing, www is at times said to stand for the Wild Wild Web.

The overload on the Web can be of all kinds. Which search service should I choose (*Search Engine overload*)? Help, I'm drowning in all the ads (*Advertisment overload*)! Sometimes it just might be too much with all the choices you have to make on the Web and all the undesired things you have to deal with. Some things to consider:

Search engines search on words, not concepts

The search engines match the entered search words with the contents on the Web pages that the search engine has indexed. No consideration is given to concepts; the matching is mechanical.

Garbage in, garbage out

The best search can never be better than the contents on the Web pages that are accessible on the Web. For certain subjects there may not be any qualitative resources on the Web, and then the search services can't deliver anything that is good.

No editors clean out

On the Web there is nobody who cleans or throws away things. What's put up on the Web remains there as long as the Web server, on which it's accessible, is running and nobody actively removes it. In modern Web-publishing systems you can often decide that a Web page will be inactive if nobody has checked it after a certain amount of time.

Know your limits

Broaden your outlooks on the Web slowly but surely. Try new search services and search on new subjects, but not on places that you can't relate to or control.

Go ahead and dive deeply into the Web sites of authorities and other organizations, but be more careful with commercial or private Web pages.

Assessment of Web pages

All Web pages have two things in common: all have a sender and all have a purpose. This leads up to two questions:

- Why – which is the purpose of the Web page?
- Who – who is the sender of the page?

Purposes

Why was the information published? Web sites can be divided into the following categories:

- Influence
- Business activity
- Information
- News
- Personal
- Entertainment

Is the purpose spelled out? Which is the purpose of the page? Which opinions are brought up on the page? Sometimes the purpose is clear, but if you're uncertain you can look under "about us" or "about the Web site" which is often located in the top menu, the left menu or in the foot of the page.

Sender

Who published the information? What do you know about the sender?

- Who wrote the page?
- What qualifications does the Web page's creator have?
- Who published the page?
- Who's responsible for the Web site?
- Is there any contact information?

To consider for the assessment

- Is the information up to date and complete?
- Is the information presented in an objective way?
- Is the document well written?
- When was the page published?
- How often is the Web site updated?
- Are there sources or references?

Source criticism

Traditional source criticism

The traditional source criticism builds on four principles and one distinction. The criteria are:

+ **Authenticity.** The source should be what it claims to be.
+ **Relationship in time.** The distance in time between the event that the source describes and the origin of the source is important from the reliability point of view.
+ **Independence.** The source should not be a copy or a summary of another source.
+ **Freedom of tendency.** The source should not be a party of anyone or anything. If the creator of the source has an interest in the case there is a big risk that the source is biased.

In traditional source criticism a distinction is made between narratives about something and the remains of something. A written agreement, for example, is a remnant of an agreement, but the agreement may, naturally, also narrate something.

Source criticism for the Internet

To the four traditional criteria described above it is possible to add three more criteria, adapted to the information on the Internet[1]:

+ World picture and approach to knowledge as bias
+ Reliability
+ Prerequisites and characteristics of the source

World picture and approach to knowledge as bias

All sources could be said to be biased, even if they don't form part of the case. All sources are products of the culture in which they were created and in which they exist. Cultures consist of religious ideas, traditions, history, language, customs, ideals and laws, and all this together can be summed up to a world picture.

To assess a source you have to determine its world picture. Via the Internet you rapidly and simply reach information from every corner in the world and from widely differing world pictures and you constantly have to take your stand in relation to biased information.

---

1 Leth, Göran & Thurén, Torsten (2000). *Källkritik för Internet [Source criticism for the Internet]*. Stockholm: Styrelsen för psykologiskt försvar [http://www.psycdef.se/Global/PDF/Publikationer/kallkritid for internet.pdf]

Reliability

The huge amount of information means that you all the time have to drop sources and only use some of all the hits you've got. But which should you pick? You may consider:

♦ Information about the creator: name, title, position, organizational affiliation, date of origin and contact information.

♦ Which domain? Commercial .com or .edu (US education) says something about the purpose of the Web site. Swedish .se doesn't mean a lot as it isn't restricted to any special category but accessible to everyone from authorities and companies to separate individuals.

♦ The address of the Web page. If the Web address is simple and without sub-directories this generally means that the Web page is the first page of the Web site, e.g., www.omis.se.

♦ Private Web address? The address www.student.lu.se/~fte99jfr/bib052/ says that it belongs to a student at Lund University. It should perhaps not be considered to be particularly reliable, unless you're one of the students at the course BIB052, the Invisible Web, where the Web page is used.

Prerequisites and characteristics of the source

No sources are perfect. Sources make mistakes (without wanting to delude or distort). Sources can't keep up, but have to restrict themselves or they don't work technically as expected. When you want to use a source you should get an idea of its prerequisites and characteristics. What is true of the source? Under which prerequisites does the source work? Who puts the information into the database and what is not included?

Enhanced source criticism – media knowledge

Today, or in any case when we're speaking of the Internet, it's become more relevant to talk about media knowledge. All knowledge about the conditions that apply to Net publishing will help you to critically assess what you find. Another important part is the conditions that control the search services that you use to get the information. Who selected the links in the Web directory? Why is this hit the number one hit in the search engine's hit list? Is it possible to see which of the links are ads?

"False" Web sites

RYT Hospital – The Dwayne Medical Center (www.rythospital.com). The Web site belongs to a fictitious hospital where, among other things, they have succeeded to bring about male pregnancy...

The Dihydrogen Monoxide Research Division (www.dhmo.org). The Web site has the same style as many pseudo-scientific sites. The information is hard to assess if you don't know anything about the subject.

Several Wikis use the Wiki software Mediawiki (freely accessible at www.mediawiki.org), among others the Wikipedia (http://wikipedia.org). But many other wikis also have the same appearance as Wikipedia, precisely because they use the same software. No other reson.

Quality control

Information in, for example, books, journals and (pay-) databases has often passed through various steps of quality control. These steps may consist of publishers, editors, fact editors and librarians who in various ways review and assess the information. On the Internet it's easier to publish information and only a small part of the information is reviewed thoroughly.

The target group of the page

The Web page's target group? Laypersons or specialists? Children or adults?

The address of the page

Can you through the Web address, the URL, know anything about the page? Today anybody can buy an .se-address (the Swedish top domain) which is why it's not any longer a sign of quality in itself. Company- or organization names may be a sign of quality, especially if the name constitutes the entire domain name, e.g., www.volvo.se. leads to the official Web page of the Volvo group, while www.volvoforum.de leads to a German discussion forum for Volvo owners.

Longish addresses with a tilde (~) in the Web address indicates a private Web page. These often lie under a big Web actor like AOL or Yahoo! where it's often free to put up Web pages. It's also common for university colleges and universities to give staff and students their own space for publication of private pages. The contents, thus, don't need to be related to the person's subject studies or research area. Just because a person is the professor of a subject he or she is not an authority in other subjects.

Similar addresses

Don't let yourself be fooled by addresses that are similar. To use a Web address that looks like a known and respected address is often a way to trick someone who has misspelt the address. It can also be a way for people who have another opinion in the subject to present this on the Net. Other people have as their purpose to make visitors enter through misspellings and with that be able to expose commercials or sponsored links. The Web site is paid for by the display of advertisements, so you could say that the business concept here is to make use of surfers who are lost and who might not discover this immediately.

Trace the owner

Trace the owner of a Web site via a WHOIS search service. WHOIS search services are used to find out who the owner of a domain is. How much information you get depends upon how the address is registered and under which domain. Sometimes you will get both the name and address to the owner.

10. The Search Services & the Market

Are the search services media companies or technique companies?

Links as commodities

Links constitute a big commodity and can be said to be of three different types:

- Link from a search engine index (to a search engine which lacks its own index, e.g., Altavista)
- Sponsored link from a special index (which is mixed into a hit list in a search service)
- Commercial link (which is presented next to the hit list in a search service or on a common Web site)

All links that the target Web site has paid for in any way are paid links. The opposite to the paid links in the search engines are called organic links and are those links that the search engine's spider collects.

The Bruce Clay Search Engine Chart (www.bruceclay.com/searchenginerelationshipchart.htm) is a service provided by the consultancy firm Bruce Clay. It's a chart where you can see what the relationships of the search engines look like. If you click on a square, a fact sheet about the search service will pop up. On the chart the red arrows denote primary search results, i.e., organic hits. Paid links are marked with yellow arrows and are delivered from the dominating actors Google and Yahoo! to the other search services.

In 2004 it was estimated that the eight largest search services handled over 600 million searches daily. Google's part was about 250 million/day. The number of searches in the search services increases steadily each year. In August 2007 the number of searches in the world was estimated to 61 billion/month (2 billion/day). Of the 61 billion searches Google is estimated to handle 60 per cent.[1] In August 2009 13.9 billion searches were conducted in the US, 64.6 percent of them in Google.[2] And the users from US are only 16.2 percent of the total amount of users world wide (over 1 billion).[3]

---

1 ComScore Press Release, October 10, 2007: http://www.comscore.com/Press_Events/Press_releases/2007/10/Worldwide_Searches_Reach_61_Billion
2 ComScore Press Release, September 22, 2009: http://www.comscore.com/Press_Events/Press_releases/2009/9/comScore_Releases_August_2009_U.S._Search_Engine_Rankings
3 ComScore Press Release, January 23, 2009: http://www.comscore.com/Press_Events/Press_releases/2009/1/Global_Internet_Audience_1_Billion

What line of business are the search engines in?

Searchers believe that the search engines are in the business of searching. Searchers rely on free, commercial search services to quickly and easily find the relevant information they want, irrespective of search query, complexity and language.

As a matter of fact, the commercial search engines are in the business of advertising. They receive their largest share of the income from delivering context-dependent ads. Bought hits, sponsored links, etc., are directed advertising.

An inquiry in 2001 showed that half of the hits in the meta search services were bought hits. Watch out!

The three big ones of the search engines

The operation of the search engines is built on three things:

- *Traffic* – more searchers mean more people who will follow the commercial links.
- *Relevance* – give meaningful answers to the searches to keep the searchers happy and make them return.
- *Monetarism* – convert the traffic to revenues through, for example, commercial links and banners.

Today the search engines need to be good at all three things mentioned above: creating traffic to the search engine, delivering good answers to the searches and making use of the traffic created to the search engine to earn money. As a searcher you should make sure that you use the search engines more than they use you.

Sponsored links, bought hits and advertising

During the last years the main emphasis has changed from pure advertising (banners and pop-up commercials) to sponsored links and bought hits.

Three types of bought hits

- Bought placing – higher up or at the side of the hit list
- Bought inclusion – somewhere among the hits
- Bought indexing – guaranteed placing in the search engine's index (or directory)

How bought hits are presented in practice

Google keeps the sponsored links outside of the hit list in a rather clear way. The sponsored links are, principally, shown to the right of the hit list. Sometimes sponsored links are also shown above the hits list but in that case they have a background colour.

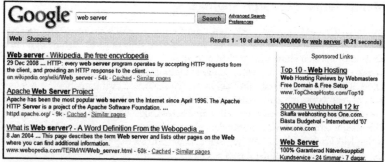

Fig. Sponsored links in Google in a search on "web server".

Google earlier used numbering of the hits in the hit list. But the numbering is removed and with that the difference between (organic) hits and sponsored links is a bit smaller.

Metacrawler (www.metacrawler.com), which is a meta search service, mixes in the sponsored links into the hit list. The sponsored links are marked with "sponsored by" before the URL and after the address you get information about where the sponsored link comes from.

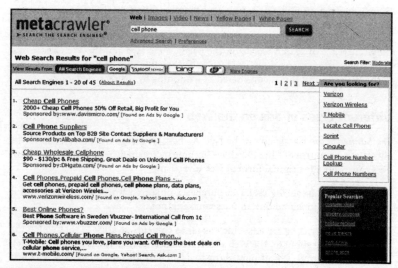

Fig. Sponsored links in Metacrawler in a search on "cell phone".

Manipulation of search engines

An entire line of business works with marketing in search services. The marketing is often connected to the optimization of Web sites or pure Web design. Two abbreviations that show up are SEM and SEO. SEM stands for *Search Engine Marketing* and SEO stands for *Search Engine Optimization*. The concepts are good to know if you want to learn more about search services. It's the people in the business of search engine optimizaiton who study the search engines in depth, which means that you sooner or later will come across SEO texts about search engines. The reason why you find the knowledge about search engines in the SEO business is that this is where there's money to make, in contrast to pure information searching where the need of consultants is small.

Search Engine Marketing as a concept includes all marketing that takes place via search services on the Net, both search engine advertising with sponsored links and search engine positioning.

Sponsored links or *bought search words* are those links that most often are shown at the side of the hit list at a search. Sometimes they are shown before the hits and sometimes they are mixed in among the organic hits. The advertiser pays the search service for each visitor who clicks on the link and the price of the link is often determined through bidding (the highest bid on top).

Search engine positioning or *search engine optimization* are different ways to improve, or optimize, a Web site so that it will get as high up as possible in the hit lists of the search engines. The optimization improves, e.g., the titles of the pages, the occurrence of search words on the pages, meta tags and the Web addresses. Sometimes external pages are used (so-called satellite sites or link farms) as links to the Web site, but this is considered as spamming by the search engines.

Different types of ads on the Web

The banner is the classic ad on the Net. A clickable image which leads on to the advertiser. In course of time they have become increasingly larger in format. Banners constitute the original form of Net advertising.

Search engine advertising refers to purchases of search words or phrases and is presented as a sponsored link in the search engines.

Contextual advertising are ads which as far as contents go stick to that which the visitor is reading about on the Web site. If the editorial material is about cars, then car ads will come up. The ad-publishing tool will look for keywords in the read text and publish dynamically relevant ads.

Behavioral advertising is based on an advertising application which stores the user's surfing. The program then presents suitable ads. The technique thus builds on the storing of personal information.

Questionable SEO solutions

Information searchers sometimes come up against questionable SEO solutions. Optimization companies are at times criticized in the press for having used for example link farms.

Link farms

A link collection on a Web page which only exists to give many incoming links to the target links is called a link farm. The links in the link farm are thought to give higher ranking in the search engines as most search engines work with link analysis. Site maps can be used as link farms.

Cloaking

To show one Web page to the search engines and another to the visitors in order to get a high ranking in the search engines is called cloaking. You hide the real page to the search engine and instead show a page with many keywords.

Door pages

An entrance page to a Web site which has been created for the sole purpose of ranking high in the search engines is called a door page. The door page is often not seen but the visitor is directly sent on to the real first page. The page is optimized for search engines and doesn't contain any information for the visitor.

Misspelt Web addresses

If you enter an incorrect URL you increasingly more often come to a page which is using the page that you intended to visit. Sometimes the page is similar to that which you were looking for with the purpose of detaining less observant users and making them click on the links. At times it's only a simple Web page with links.

11. The Invisible Web

The Invisible Web is hard to define. Several similar concepts are used for its designation. *The Invisible Web* was coined by a researcher in 1994 for that which wasn't visible to the search engines. *The Hidden Web* is used as a synonym to the Invisible Web. Some people consider that the Invisible Web as a concept is misleading as nothing is invisible, only hidden. The company BrightPlanet introduced *The Deep Web* in 2000 to focus more on techniques that make the information in databases visible.

The relevance of the Invisible Web

The Invisible Web is becoming increasingly relevant as a concept for many reasons. Both the number of visitors and the share of those who choose to use a search engine for their searches are growing – more people than ever are affected by the Invisible Web. The awareness of the Invisible Web has grown; both among searchers and information producers, and more information sources have become visible. Most people who search for information use search services. The information that can't be found in the search services can then be thought of as invisible, as it's unfindable by the search services.

At the same time the Web is growing faster than the search engines' indexes – the growth on the Net results in the largest part of the information remaining invisible. Other information sources than pure Web pages are added at a hurried pace: sound, image, video, podcasts, news, e-books, e-journals, discussion lists, blogs, RSS flows, wikis. The search engines only include a few file types other than html, principally those with text-based information.

The search engines give an idea of the Web which is about a month old in average. It takes time and resources for search engines to re-visit Web pages. The average time is estimated to one month.

More and better hybrid search services which do searches in the Deep Web are being introduced. Still, these are principally technical solutions which are sold for use within companies. But also the traditional search engines are including increasingly more material from the Deep Web.

A number of different reasons as to why the Invisible Web is important to all who search for information on Net were presented here. An awareness of the Invisible Web is required to ensure really efficient searches.

What is the Invisible Web?

A short definition would be: *Everything which the search engines can't see.* Meaning all the information which the search engines can't include in their indexes and with that make it searchable. But it's more complex than that. The concept of the Invisible Web departs from the search engines, not from us as information seekers or from the Web as a whole.

What the Invisible Web actually is would be something that shifts constantly depending on:

Which search engine it is

As the Invisible Web is search-engine dependent it's different for each search engine.

What the search engine indexes

The search engines have somewhat different coverage, i.e., they index somewhat different parts of the Web.

How the search engine does the indexing

A search engine won't always include the whole text or all images on a Web page. That which is excluded will be invisible at searches.

How often the search engine re-indexes its pages

Popular Web pages are generally re-visited more often by the search engines, but it's up to each search engine.

How big an index the search engine has

The numbers of Web pages that the search engines have indexed differ greatly. A smaller index means that more things are invisible.

What file types the search engine indexes

In addition to Web pages search engines may index other file types such as PDF, DOC or Flash. But the search engines are restrictive when it comes to which file type they will index and how big a part of the files they will include in their index.

The rapid growth of the Web

The Web is constantly growing and at a hurried pace. The search engines can't keep up and at the same time have a fresh index. And it can take weeks for a new Web page to become indexed.

What does the Invisible Web contain?

The Invisible Web contains texts, files and other information which is not indexed by the search engines, due to technical reasons or because of selections that the seach engine makes.

Many databases are accessible via the Web. Their contents can in most cases be regarded as forming part of the Invisible Web.

In databases which are reachable via the Web, but which most often are invisible in the search engines, you find:

+ telephone numbers
+ patents
+ laws
+ definitions of words
+ things for sale in Web stores or Web auctions
+ product information
+ digital exhibitions and galleries
+ graphic- and sound files
+ new and variable information
+ news
+ job ads
+ available airplane tickets, hotel rooms etc.
+ stock-exchange rates, prices for bonds, currency rates etc.
+ essays and degree theses

Reasons for invisibility

The Invisible Web consists of documents on the Web which the large search engines can't or don't want to index for different reasons. Partly because of technical reasons, many things are hard or impossible to index, partly because of financial reasons. Each indexed page requires a little bit of the search engine's computer capacity. Perhaps it requires too much to index a certain Web site in proportion to how interesting it is to the search engine users. Space costs money. But also strategic reasons exist to attract more searchers and not lose the ones you already have.

Different technical reasons
+ Unlinked pages – no link for the search engine spider to follow to the page. The page turns into an island on the Web.
+ Pages that principally consist of images, sound or video – not enough text for the search engine to "understand" what the page is about results in the ignoring of the page.
+ Real time information – short-lived data; enormous quantities; rapidly changeable, like stock-exchange rates; radio- and TV emissions.

- Contents in relation databases – the spider can't fill in the fields or in other ways make the choices that are required for the database to search for information.
- Dynamically generated contents – adapated contents are irrelevant to most searchers. Here is also a fear of "spider traps" on the part of the search engines, places where the spider can get caught without being able to move on.

What can't or won't the search engines index?

- Not entire documents if they're big. The search engines generally have an upper limit where they stop indexing the documents. Google's limit was earlier 101 kB. This is the explanation to why cached pages can end abruptly.
- Not all so-called stop words like *to* and *and* can be excluded to save space. Since more and more search engines save complete pages, the earlier excluded stop words are now also included.
- Not all meta data. E.g., not the information in the head of the page, between <head> ... <\head> which earlier was used, among other things, to indicate misleading keywords in the meta tags with the purpose of manipulating the search engines.
- Not all directories at a Web site. The search engines often delimit how deeply they will index in the directory structure (e.g., not all the way down to www.omis/filer/dokument/2005/december/lista.html).

Advantages with the Invisible Web

In the Invisible Web there are no personal homepages and no commercial advertising (yet). The contents are, to a great extent, produced by different institutions and often with a specific purpose. The broad, general information is not published here but on visible Web sites. This saves time for the searcher (if you know what you're looking for) and the risk of using "bad" information becomes smaller. You're also spared sales and commercials, something that can take time and that generates a lot of noise (if you're not looking for products or services).

Different types of Invisible Web

The Invisible Web can be divided into different parts:

- The poorly ranked Web
- The un-indexed Web
- The private Web
- The protected Web
- The really invisible Web
- The fresh Web
- The disappearing Web

◆   The non-existent Web

The poorly ranked Web

Much information in the search engines is practically invisible as it's ranked low in the search engines' hit lists; the information can be said to be buried far down in the hit list.

◆   Unusual file types, everything that's not a normal Web page, often end up far down in the hit list.

◆   Limitations in the number of hits shown. All search engines have a limitation in the number of shown hits. You can often see only a couple of hundred of hits, even if the search has generated 3 million hits.

◆   Fresh Web pages that are linked to by few others (few inlinks) receive a lower value in the ranking than those linked to by important Web sites or by many (many/important inlinks).

How you search the poorly ranked Web

◆   Change search words or use synonyms – substitute search words or use OR. In Google the tilde (~) is used.

◆   Change the order of the search words. The search words are weighted differently when the relevance is estimated.

◆   Double the most important search word to increase its weight at the relevance estimation (works in Google, Yahoo! and Exalead).

◆   Repeat the search in different search services – they have different coverage and ranking.

◆   Search for different types of information, sound, image etc. with the special functions of the search services or in search services for specific file types.

◆   Think about in what format you may easier find the information. Perhaps it's presented in reports (PDF) or as presentations (PPT) – limit your search to a specific file type.

The un-indexed Web

Consists of files which could be included in the search engines' indexes but which aren't. This part of the Invisible Web is extensive and hard to find. A large part of the Web is un-indexed.

Different reasons are:

◆   The indexing depth
◆   The indexing frequency
◆   Unlinked pages
◆   Badly designed Web pages (search engine unfriendly)

To test whether a page is indexed in Google you write *info:* before the Web address:

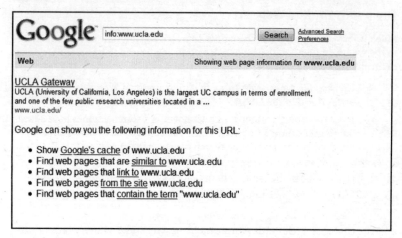

Fig. Info:www.ucla.edu i Google.

The page is indexed and you can choose among the following:

♦ Look at the version in Google cache. (The page is saved as it was when Google last visited/indexed the page).

♦ Let Google do a search for pages that look like the page of interest.

♦ See which pages link to the page of interest.

♦ Look at the pages from the site www.ucla.edu.

♦ Let Google do a search for pages that contain the URL of the page of interest.

If you look for info: for a page which isn't indexed you only get the following choices:

♦ Go to the address of interest.

♦ Let Google do a search for pages that contain the page's URL.

A page which isn't indexed:

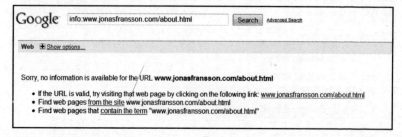

Fig. Info:www.jonasfransson.com/about.html i Google.

How you search the un-indexed Web
- ◆ Subject directories
- ◆ Industry portals
- ◆ Go directly to where the information may be found
- ◆ Test different search engines (different coverage on the Web)

The private Web

Web site owners can in different ways prevent search engines from indexing Web pages. A Web editor has three ways in which to exclude a page from a search engine:

- ◆ To use passwords which protect the page so that a search engine spider can't get passed the form.
- ◆ To use robots.txt to prevent spiders from getting to the page (the Web Robots Pages, www.robotstxt.org/wc/robots.html).
- ◆ To use the meta tag "noindex" which prevents the spider from reading the rest of the page and from indexing the page.

Web pages in the private Web can have different purposes. Perhaps these are family pages which are intended for use only by family and friends. They might also be pages for a project that originally had a specific target group. Or a Web site under construction.

Increasingly more often it's required that you enter a code consisting of four, five letters and numbers shown in a somewhat distorted image box next to the box where you have to enter the code. This is a simple password which protects the service from being utilized by automatized programs, like the search engine spiders. It has to be a human being who reads and enters the code and with that use the service. Other passwords for search engines work in the same way – like a blind alley.

How you search the private Web
- ◆ Subjecct directories
- ◆ Industry portals
- ◆ Indirectly in search engines

The protected Web

In the protected Web, as in the private Web, the search engines are prevented from indexing the contents. The protected Web is more commercial to its nature, it's often about tying up users to make them return or pay for the services.

- ◆ Pages where the user has to agree to certain terms to get access to the page.

- In many cases the Web pages are freely accessible after registration.
- In other cases a fee is charged, per page or as some kind of subscription.
- Traditional database companies are also included here (e.g. Dialog, www.dialog.com).

How you search the protected Web
- Industry portals
- Register as a user at separate, free Web sites
- Searching in pay services – subscription or pay for separate searches

The really invisible Web

The really invisible Web is the large amount of information that is stored in databases and unusual file formats. With modern technique a lot can be indexed, but to a great extent today's search engines build on techniques from the birth of the Web (first half of the 1990's).

- The Web sites which the search engines can't index for technical reasons.
- The file formats which the spider isn't programmed to handle.
- Difficult for the search engine to categorize owing to a small amount of text. All searching in the search engines takes place through matching of search words to words on the Web page. If the Web page contains few words the page may become unfindable in the index.
- The search engines have chosen not to index the pages.
- Dynamic pages – poorly constructed pages can turn into spider traps, i.e., the search engine spider gets trapped in the generated links and can't move on.
- Information in relation databases – a question to the database is required.

How you search the really invisible Web
- Indirecly in search engines (e.g. for databases)
- Directories
- Industry portals

The fresh Web

There's a constant publishing going on on the Web. News, blog contributions, press releases, new Web pages, reports etc.. One part of this is indexed practically immediately by the large search engines, but a lot of information remains invisible for weeks or months.

How you search the fresh Web
- News search services

- Blog search services
- Via experts' Web pages
- Monitoring subject or Web site – passive searching

The disappearing Web

The Web is not static, but developing and changing constantly. Information is added and disappears – *"here today, gone tomorrow."*

How you search the disappearing Web

- Cut the URL to get to a working Web page in order to start searching onwards again.
- Check the URL in a search engine using *cache:*
- Do a Web site search in a search engine with keywords from the disappeared page (*site:*).
- If 1-3 don't work, or if the entire Web site has disappeared, try the Internet Archive (www.archive.org).

The disappeared information can be sought after in Web archive services, see the Old Web.

The non-existent Web

EVERYTHING is not on the Web! People may often be the key to the information you're looking for. If your search doesn't result in anything, in spite of your efforts – look for an expert.

How you search the non-existent Web

- Check with friends or colleagues. Perhaps someone knows about a good starting-point or an important resource. Many organizations have an "information guru" or information function.
- Contact a public library near by – professional help for free.
- Consult a researcher.

The Deep Web

The company BrightPlanet divides the Web into two parts, the Surface Web and the Deep Web. They consider that *the Deep Web* is a more correct concept than the Invisible Web.

The Surface Web is the static Web pages that the search engines can reach, and which thereby become visible and searchable in the traditional search engines. Under the surface lie the dynamically generated Web pages and the databases which the search engines can't reach, which is why the Deep Web becomes hidden or invisible.

Most of the information on the Web is buried in dynamically generated Web pages, which don't exist until they're created as the answer to a specific search.

The size of the Deep Web

In 2001 the company BrightPlanet estimated the Web's size to 7500 terabytes. More numbers from the report:[1]

*   The Superfical Web: 19 terabytes and 1 billion documents (1 terabyte = 1000 gigabytes).
*   The Deep Web: 7500 terabytes and 550 billion documents.
*   The Deep Web is 400-550 times bigger than the Superficial Web.
*   The Deep Web contains 1000-2000 times more quality information than the Superficial Web.

Google has estimated the content on the Internet to 5 million TB, whereof Google had indexed 170 TB (a thirty-thousandth part) in October 2005.[2]

If the content on the Internet has doubled to 10 million TB totally since Google's estimation and if the Deep Web is 500 times bigger than the Superficial Web, then the Superfical Web is 20 000 TB and the Deep Web almost 10 million TB. If Google has doubled its index in the meantime they have indexed about 350 TB, almost 2 per cent of the Superficial Web.

On the other hand there are researchers who claim that Google has indexed 76 per cent of the indexable Web (the Superficial Web) which is estimated to consist of minimum 11.5 billion Web pages (2005).[3]

The content of the Deep Web

*   The content of the Deep Web is relevant to each information need.
*   More than half of the content is found in subject-specific databases.
*   95 % of the Deep Web is freely accessible information – neither fees nor subscriptions.

The greatest part of the content is according to BrightPlanet subject databases (54 %). Together with documents on Web sites and archived publications the subject databases make up incredible amounts of subject-specific information and make up close to 80 % of the Deep Web. Trade-related Web sites, like auction sites, represent about 10 % of the content. Some other parts are portals (3 %) and libraries (2 %). The study was done in 2001 so the proportions may have changed somewhat, but the numbers offer an image of the Deep Web.

1 The 'Deep' Web: Surfacing Hidden Value (http://www.brightplanet.com/component/content/article/23-details/119-the-deep-web-surfacing-hidden-value.html)
2 Softpedia: How Big is the Internet? (http://news.softpedia.com/news/How-Big-Is-the-Internet-10177.shtml)
3 Gulli, A. & Signorini, A. (2005) The indexable web is more than 11.5 billion pages. (http://doi.acm.org/10.1145/1062745.1062789)

The Invisible Web and the Deep Web

You can combine the Invisible Web and the Deep Web. The illustration below is an attempt to make clear the relations between the two concepts. The Invisible Web is search-engine dependent, whereas the Deep Web departs from the nature of the information and how this is stored.

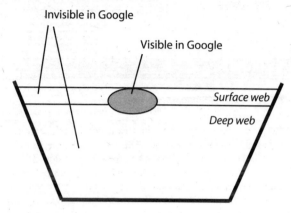

Fig. Visible and invisible in Google.

The proportions in the image show the possible different relations between what is visible and what is invisible, or, in other words, how much is indexed in the search engines, in this case Google, and how much isn't.

The Old Web

The growth on the Web is over 200 per cent per year. At the same time about 40 per cent disappears yearly, of which a part is of historical interest.

Through the Internet Archive and the Waybackmachine (www.archive.org) you can search for old Web pages.

You find an alternative entrance to the Internet Archive and the Waybackmachine at the Web site of the Alexandria Library (it may be needed at times when the other one is slow): www.bibalex.org/English/initiatives/internetarchive/about.htm

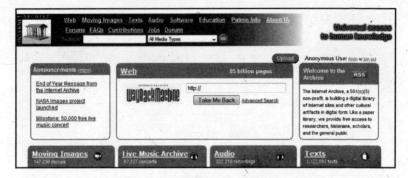

Fig. The Internet Archive and the Waybackmachine

Search engines with cached versions of the indexed Web pages in their search engine indexes can also be used to retrieve lost pages. This is only possible, however, if the search engine hasn't had time to return to the Web page to re-index the page. The sometimes slow re-indexing is the answer to the question why it's not always the same page that you see as cached in the search engine and which you later come to. If it comes to the worst, the Web page will have changed completely from the point of view of content since the search engine last paid a visit.

Searching the Invisible Web

When should you search the Deep/Invisible Web?

- When you're looking for dynamic and changeable information, like news, job ads or flight departures.
- When you want to find information that is normally stored in a database.
- When you want to search beyond the limited index of the search engines.

Different search services for searching the Invisible Web

Search services
- Invisible Web gateways
- Directories/subject directories
- Search engines and specialized search engines
- At the source (database searches)

Invisible Web gateways
Pronounced focus on the Invisible Web

- CompletePlanet (www.completeplanet.com) – directory

- IncyWincy (www.incywincy.com) – search engine

Directories/subject directories
- The Librarians' Internet Index (http://lii.org) – try searching on *database* to find database, combine with subject words.
- Infomine (http://infomine.ucr.edu)

Search engines and specialized search engines
- Google, Yahoo!, Bing, ... – e.g., try *migration database*
- Google News (http://news.google.com)
- Blinkx (www.blinkx.com) – video search engine
- Picsearch (www.picsearch.com) – image search engine

To find search services similar to a known one, try *related:* in Google. A search for related:www.picsearch.com returns a bunch of image search services.

Search strategies

Search words which point you in the right direction
If you don't search in services which are specific for the Invisible Web, you have to select search words that point in the direction of the invisible material that you're after:

- *database + subject word*
- *archive + subject word*
- *search* ("click here to search", points to database)
- *listen* (points to sound file) in Google: *elvis listen*

Search for databases
The information in the Invisible Web is generally found in databases that you can reach via the Web. In spite of the fact that the search engines can't search in the databases they can locate the homepages or search forms of many databases.

When you search for databases you should use your search words/subject words together with words like *database*, *archive* and *repository*. For example:

"plane crash" AND database

File type
The limiting of your search to a certain file type may result in valuable material, e.g.:

"invisible web" and limit the file type to PPT (Power Point)

Search for places where the content of the Invisible Web is likely to be

Figure out how you can reach the page with the information indirectly. Which page may link to the information you're looking for? Interest groups and authorities are good starting points.

Indirect search – two-step search

Which Web site may contain what you're looking for? The search engines don't index (include in their databases) all the pages, not the complete pages and not all the images and links. But you can find a lot of things indirectly through the search engines.

Inverted link search

When you've found a database usable for the Invisible Web you should make use of other users who have found the resource to be good when it comes to locating other Web sites. Through inverted link searching you can find directories and link collections which link to the database you're interested in. They also often link to other good resources.

link:http://www.planecrashinfo.com

will give Web pages that link to www.planecrashinfo.com and which are included in the index of the search engine.

Make use of the search tools of the Web sites

Databases are often "hidden" far down at Web sites. To find them you should use the search tools of big authoritative Web sites, e.g. the UN, the World Bank or the big universities.

Look through your bookmarks

Perhaps you've already found a good Web site for the Invisible Web and saved a bookmark. How do you know that a bookmarked Web site belongs to the Invisible Web? Use the "URL test" to check it. Place the cursor to the left of a question mark in a URL in the browser's address box and erase everything to the right, including the question mark, and then reload the page. If you get an error message or "the page could not be found" it's probably a resource to the Invisible Web as the whole address was needed in order for the database to create a meaningful page.

Monitor subject-specific e-mail lists or forums

Find e-mail lists or forums where subject experts or information specialists such as librarians and journalists carry on discussions. Follow the discussions or search the archive if there is one. Much of the knowledge and the experiences that pass these channels will never be printed (or be up on the Web).

Limit your search to specific file types

By limiting your search in a search engine to one file type it will be easier to find material of more content.

filetype:ppt "invisible web" OR "deep web"

Search in specialized search engines

Specialized search engines often index deeper at relevant Web sites or in entire PDF files (both Google and Yahoo! have had limitations in the number of kB that is indexed.

At the source – example travel planners

Some bus- and train companies may have travel planners, services on the Web where you can find information about stops, routes and timetables by searching on point of departure and destination. The information is invisible in an ordinary search engine. It's not possible to enter the destination of your journey and means of travel in a search engine, e.g., *bus lund copenhagen* and get the next relevant bus departure. Some companies publish their timetables in PDF format, so search words like *timetable Stockholm pdf* can lead you to timetables.

Searchability of images in search engines

To search for images is harder as the search engines base their operations on text and signs. The following normally applies:

- The file name is indexed, e.g., leo12.jpg.
- The ALT tag can be indexed if it exists.
- Text which is close to the image is often indexed.

This means that you should search on 1-3 search words when you search for images, not more.

Google Image Search: search on *boeing 747* and *747 boeing* in two different windows and compare the hit lists. What you get is more or less the same hits but with different ranking owing to the order of the search words. (See the illustration in Chapter 2).

Remember the copyright! Most images that you find on the Web are owned by someone.

12. Databases

What is a database?

From the user perspective a database is often a large amount of information, collected in a closed system. As a user you can often search in separate databases but only the owner of the database can publish the information in the database. On the Web, however, everybody can easily publish his or her own information.

The tradiational databases existed long before the Web came into existence and they were earlier accessible in other ways, e.g., through a direct connection with a modem. The databases that you meet today on the Net have a so-called Web interface which makes it possible to search the database via the Web.

In contrast to the search engines, the information in the databases is not put there entirely automatically; the input takes place under controlled forms and is done by editors. The image below illustrates the fact that editors do the input in the index which together with the interface makes up the database.

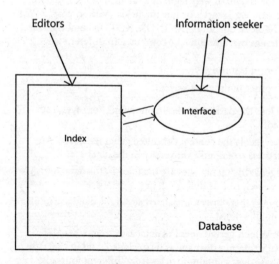

Fig. The structure of a traditional database. Compare to the structure of the search engines in Chapter 2.

Databases are important tools when it comes to efficient searches for information. Common types of databases are:

- **Library directories** which show what literature there is at one or several libraries
- **Reference database** which give references to literature (e.g., journal articles or scientific reports), sometimes they contain abstracts, short summaries of the contents
- **Fact databases** which contain facts, not references, e.g., statistics and encyclopaedias
- **Full-text databases** which contain complete texts, e.g., scientific journal articles.

Characteristics of the databases

The database is restocked by editors

This makes for a selected and controlled content. The form in which the information is stored is also fixed. Clear fields are filled in with meta-information (information about information) in a standardized manner. In many databases a controlled vocabulary (subject words) is also used which makes it easier to find everything in a specific subject.

Controlled searches can be done

By having the content in the database well regulated, as to its form, controlled searches are possible. You can, e.g., search in specific fields (author, year...). You can normally also use the Boolean operators (AND, OR, NOT) to combine search words. Advanced search strings can also often be combined in different ways.

Differences between different databases

Databases differ from each other in different ways:

- Subject content: Does the database contain one subject or several subjects closely related?
- Geographical coverage: Is the content delimited geographically? Are there, e.g., only articles from Lund University in the database?
- Linguistic coverage: Which languages are included in the database? Are there, e.g., only research results in English in the database?
- Types of material: Are there only journal articles in the database or also books and other publications?
- Different periods: Which period does the database cover, when did the collecting of information start and is it concluded, and in that case when? If the database, e.g., contains articles from different journals, when did the indexing of each separate journal begin?

A database can be accessible in different ways, freely on the Web and through different database companies (one example is Thomson at www.thomson.com).

The database companies make the database accessible through their platforms and consequently you can find great differences when it comes to interface and functionality.

Choice of database

Many factors determine the choice of database:

- Which information is needed: books, journal articles or articles from the daily papers?
- How much time do you have to your disposal to get the material?
- Are you looking for Swedish or international contexts?
- Language limitations – only in Swedish?
- Should the material be scientific?
- Access to the database?

Example of database: ERIC

ERIC stands for the Education Resources Information Center and contains bibliographic information, i.e., a reference database which doesn't contain any full texts. The posts in ERIC describe articles and books and each post includes subject words and short abstracts, a short description of the content.

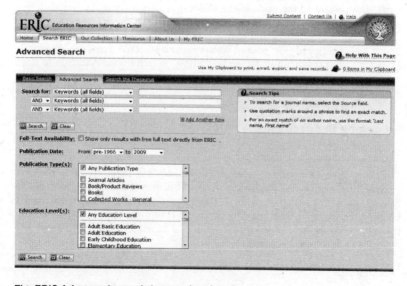

Fig. ERIC Advanced search (www.eric.ed.gov)

The database has a pedagogical content but also includes closely related research areas as, e.g., information science.

ERIC is accessible both via traditional database suppliers (e.g., Dialog) and freely on the Web (www.eric.ed.gov). ERIC is a US database, funded by public means.

Comparison traditional database – search engine

In comparison to a traditional database the search engines perform an extensive collecting of data, which takes place automatically and which is therefore relatively uncontrolled. In the databases the collecting of data is done by human beings who follow certain stipulated rules.

The search engines use advanced retrieval technique and complex relevance estimation (see Chapter 2), everything to be able to present as good a hit list as possible. But this leads to less control for the user. In the databases things are often the other way around, there is no advanced relevance estimation. In the databases the hit list is often presented in alphabetical order or by date and in many cases you can select a sorting order. But most of the structuring and the selections are left to the user, which is why subject words are particularly important for searches in databases. To search with subject words is a way to guarantee certain relevance in the search results.

In a reference database you search in the database for information about the information, the search is done in standardized information about articles and reports. The content in the posts of the database may entirely lack a linguistic resemblance to the document of interest; the content will be presented in a uniform way through subject words and abstract. In the index of the search engines you search entirely or partly for indexed Web pages and other file types, i.e., you search "directly" in the information. When searching in search engines you have to start out from what's on the Web page or in the document instead of using carefully structured posts as your point of departure.

Searching in databases

Subject vocabulary or thesaurus

Databases often have subject vocabularies accessible in their database. The lists present the controlled subject words which the editors use for description of the content when they put up the posts. A thesaurus is a word list where the relations between the words are defined. The thesaurus is in most cases hierarchical, i.e., the subject words are divided into inferior and superior concepts. In English a controlled subject word is called a *descriptor*.

Search words

When the database is selected it's time to define your search query using words that narrow down the subject. It's important to think of the folllowing things:

- Are there synonyms or words which are much alike?

- Is the search word too specific or too general? The search word needs to relate to the content in the database; the search word *Internet* is perhaps too common in a database containing computer-scientific texts.
- Is the word spelled correctly? Are there any alternative spellings?
- Is singular or plural used?
- Is there any subject vocabulary or thesaurus in the database? Look in the description of the database, there will probably be a link to the subject vocabulary or the thesaurus.

Subject words

Subject words from the subject vocabulary or the thesaurus are always to prefer. In a thesaurus each subject word is described in a post. The subject word is briefly explained in something called a *scope note*. Words that are superior and inferior in relation to the looked-up word are included, together with closely related subject words. Also earlier used subject words which have now been replaced by the new subject word are included.

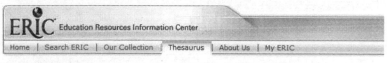

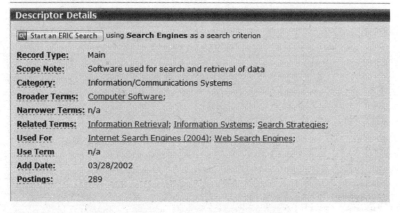

Fig. The subject word "search engines" in ERIC's thesaurus.

In the post above the subject word *search engines* is described in ERIC's thesaurus. *Search engines* is added as a subject word in 2002 and is now used instead of the earlier subject words *internet search engines* and *web search engines*.

You should always look in the subject word index/thesaurus to see which term is preferred. And, if possible, use the subject word field for your search.

EJ755251 - Who's Afraid of Google?

‹ Back to Search Results   0 items in My Clipboard | Add record to My Clipboard

Record Details

Full-Text Availability Options:

Help Finding Full Text | Find in a Library | Publisher's Web Site

Related Items: Show Related Items

Click on any of the links below to perform a new search

ERIC #:	EJ755251
Title:	Who's Afraid of Google?
Authors:	Avet, Traci
Descriptors:	Internet; Information Seeking; Search Strategies; Library Services; Online Searching
Source:	Library Journal, v131 n10 p154 Jun 2006
Peer-Reviewed:	No
Publisher:	Reed Business Information. 360 Park Avenue South, New York, NY 10010. Tel: 800-446-6551; Tel: 646-746-6400; e-mail: subsmail@reedbusiness.com; Web site: http://www.reedbusiness.com/us.html
Publication Date:	2006-06-01
Pages:	2
Pub Types:	Journal Articles; Reports - Descriptive
Abstract:	Exploring resources in order to determine their full potential in information-seeking is a necessary part of the ongoing education and training of information professionals. One should explore every resource available in order to make the best judgments when relevant queries are introduced. In this article, the author stresses that one key to great information service is to provide the needed information in a timely and effective manner. The information on the Internet holds plenty of reliable answers, or answer-leads, that patrons are seeking. Google indexes the results according to the search terms used, how the sites are written. To ignore Google's resourcefulness is to ignore a potentially useful--and thus valuable--resource at one's fingertips.
Abstractor:	ERIC
Reference Count:	0

Note:	N/A
Identifiers:	N/A
Record Type:	Journal
Level:	N/A
Institutions:	N/A
Sponsors:	N/A
ISBN:	N/A
ISSN:	ISSN-0363-0277
Audiences:	N/A
Languages:	English
Education Level:	N/A

Fig. A post in ERIC.

Study the posts

Study the appearance of the posts, their structure and content. In the image above, a post in the database ERIC is shown. The fields in the database are to the left. Of particular interest is the third field, *descriptors*, where you find the post's subject words. In the example below the title is *Who's Afraid of Google* and the article has the subject words: *Internet, Information Seeking, Search Strategies, Library Services* and *Online Searching*. Through the abstracts written about the article you can get an idea of the contents.

Free-text searching – field searching

In databases you can normally choose between doing a free-text search, i.e., a search in all fields, or do a field search, a search in a specific field, e.g., the title. If you search in the title field you will only get hits for the documents whose titles contain the search word, not all the documents which deal with the subject. You can do field searches also in search engines on the Web. Through the search syntax of the search engine you can do a search merely on the title of the Web page. In Google you write *title:anatomical*, if you want pages with *anatomical* in the title. With a free-text search you will get more hits in a database, but the number of bad hits also increases. Choose to search in specific fields as far as possible; the precision of the hits will increase. Are you looking for material *about* or *by* Astrid Lindgren?

Truncation

Truncation means to search on different endings of a word stem. Usually you add * or ? to the word stem. Specific information can be found in the help texts of the databases.

*Example: search** gives hits on:
search
searcher
searching
etc.

Truncation may give large amounts of hits, but in combination with other search words and search limitations truncation is an efficient tool.

Subject words in databases

In databases special words, so-called subject words, are used to describe the contents of the documents. The subject words may be ranged in a system, in a thesaurus, where the words are also grouped into levels of superior and inferior terms. The subject words provide one way of finding information in a subject. In order to find out which words are used in the database you're working with you can go into the subject vocabulary and have a look. There you may also find references to other words instead of the one you've looked up.

One example is an article about farms in Kronoberg in the 14th century. It can take the subject words: farms, 14th century, Middle Ages, history, Kronoberg, Småland, Götaland and Sweden.[1]

One way of searching through the use of subject words is to observe what subject words a good hit contains and then use the same subject words for further searches—this should result in similar hits.

---

1 Kronoberg, Småland and Götaland are designations of different geographical areas in southern Sweden.

13. Other Information Sources

Facts services

You might use the term facts services for the type of Web sites that function as encyclopaedias. These are not search services in the common sense of the term as they don't lead on to other Web sites. As further reading they may offer links, but their main function is to provide information. The information is in most cases self-produced (or collaborative when it comes to Wikis) and the services are not navigators but producers of information.

Wiki Web sites

Wiki Web sites, Wikis, are Web sites where the visitor can do his or her own editing of pages.

- Wikipedia (http://wikipedia.org) exists in several languages
- Webopedia (www.webopedia.com) contains Internet- and computer terms

The quality of content in Wikis is sometimes discussed. It's in their nature to be self-corrective; if anyone writes something that is incorrect this is often quickly corrected by somebody else. The risk of quality deficiencies is biggest when it comes to unusual subjects which are read by few people or in Wikis where few people edit the text. One of the strengths of the Wikis is that they can be updated quickly as this doesn't require any special decision process or payment to a writer; an active member can go in and do the editing immediately.

Ordinary Web sites

- HowStuffWorks (www.howstuffworks.com)
- How Products Are Made (www.madehow.com)
- The CIA World Factbook (https://www.cia.gov/library/publications/the-world-factbook/)
- The Internet Movie Database, IMDB (www.imdb.com)

Dictionaries

- OneLook (www.onelook.com)
- WhatIs.com (http://whatis.techtarget.com) Searchable directory of IT terms. Good descriptions and references to related terms.
- NetLingo (www.netlingo.com) Internet dictionary which also contains slangwords and slang expressions.

- TechEncyclopedia (www.techweb.com/encyclopedia/) More than 20 000 words.

Question-answering services

Question-answering services are services where you ask questions and receive answers. There are two types of question-answering services. There are communicative services, e.g., Yahoo! Answers, based on communication between people and there are mechanical question-answering services, e.g., Brainboost, which try to understand the semantics on the pages and which extract the text from the Web pages.

At the Swedish Ask The Library (www.fragabiblioteket.se/default_eng.asp) you can ask questions via forms, mail or chat and get answers from a librarian. The service also exists for children and you can ask questions in twelve languages besides Swedish. The public library part of Ask The Library is manned by about 70 public libraries while about 20 research libraries are behind the research library part.

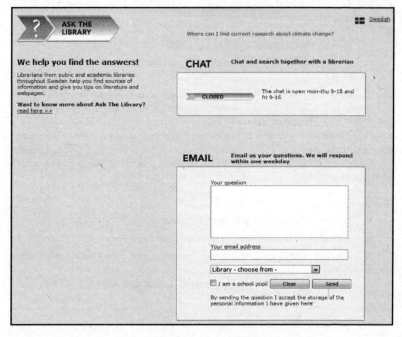

Fig. Ask The Library (www.fragabiblioteket.se/default_eng.asp).

Lists of question-answering services

♦ Ask an Expert, list at the Open Directory Project (http://www.dmoz. org/Reference/Ask_an_Expert)

♦ Ask an Expert, list at Yahoo Directory (http://d3.dir.ac2.yahoo.com/ Reference/Ask_an_Expert/)

Yahoo! has a service where other users answer the questions, Yahoo! Answers (http://answers.yahoo.com). Today the service is based on the voluntary input of separate individuals.

Fig. Yahoo! Answers where everybody can ask and answer questions.

Another variant is Brainboosts Answer Engine (www.brainboost.com). Questions are asked in normal language, e.g., *Who was Astrid Lindgren?*, and the "answer engine" provides answers from a number of Web sources. Brainboost converts the question into several searches, "reads" the hit lists and then answers the question. A similar, though simpler, function is Google's command *define:* (should be entered into the search box with a search word following directly after) which gives definitions of the search word from a number of Web resources.

Fig. Brainboost *answers the questions via text analysis.*

Other question-answering services are:

- Yedda (http://yedda.com)
- Askville (http://askville.amazon.com)

A new search service is Wolfram Alpha (www.wolframalpha.com). It calls itself a "computational knowledge engine" and can be described as a combination between a question-answering service and a fact service. Wolfram Alpha tries to answer questions by searching in different databases and then it computes and presents an answer. The search service works, right now, best when searching for facts and statistics.

Blogs

What is a blog?

Blog is an abridgment of *Web log*. A logbook on the Web. A short definition would be: A Web page that contains brief and cronologically arranged pieces of information.

A blog may contain everything from links to other Web sites to long reflections. Possibilities are often given for commenting on the entries to create a discussion.

Characteristic of blogs is:

+ Last entry comes first
+ Often updated
+ Links to Internet resources
+ Readers' comments

A blog can have different forms, everything from a personal diary to an editorial writer's debate contributions. Blogs are merely a particular type of Web site and may have just any content. In the beginning of blogging, in most cases separate individuals were behind the blogs. But nowadays groups blog increasingly more often in a theme blog. Generally speaking you can divide the blogs into two categories:

+ Professional, concerning a subject field
+ Personal, by a separate individual (e.g., about clothes)

Blogs are often used to

+ bring forth and summarize useful material
+ contextualize information by placing it in relation to information from other sources
+ give perspectives regarding major world events that traditional media miss

What is required to create a blog? Access to the Internet, certain computer skills and some Internet skills.

In the blog services on the Web the only thing required is, generally, a registration. Then you just have to follow the instructions, no knowledge of, e.g., HTML is required. But for modifications of the template and similar things adjustments of the HTML code are needed.

The Blogosphere

The Blogosphere is the denomination of the community of blogs which has developed on the Internet. The blogs comment and link to each other, forming a network.

To search for blogs

Google blog search (http://blogsearch.google.com) is one useful search service.

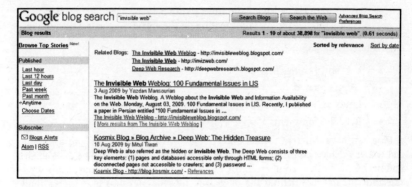

Fig. A search in Google blog search on the "Invisible Web".

Technorati (www.technorati.com) is one of the oldest blog search services.

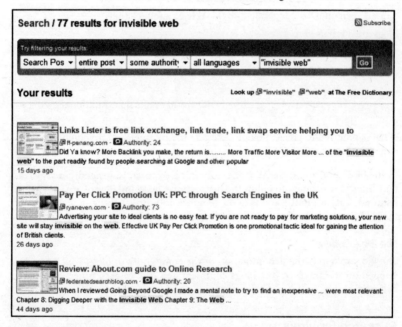

Fig. A search in Technorati on the "invisible web".

More blog search services:

- Ask (www.ask.com/?tool=bls)
- Clusty (http://blogs.clusty.com/)
- Icerocket (http://blogs.icerocket.com)

Do a search on a subject plus something that refers to blogs. One way of doing this is to search on parts of the address to a blog service:

site:blogspot.com
inurl:spaces.live.com
"spaces.live.com"

Another way is to use a standard phrase automatically generated by the service:

"powered by blogger"
"blog at wordpress.com"

Blog directories
- EatonWeb (http://portal.eatonweb.com)
- Blogorama (www.blogarama.com)
- Blogcatalog (www.blogcatalog.com)

Forums, e-mail lists and groups

Forums, e-mail lists and similar things represent one of the more interactive aspects of the Internet. Users communicate, chat and discuss.

The basic difference between groups and e-mail lists lies in how the information is mediated. In forums and in groups the messages are posted in computer networks so anyone can read them. In ordinary e-mail lists the information only goes to the members of the list.

Both the groups and the e-mail lists can be *moderated* or *unmoderated*. In unmoderated lists the mail is sent directly from the sender to all the members of the list. The mails are not examined or approved. In moderated lists it's the opposite, the list moderator controls all the mails before they are sent on to the members of the list. The control is often about keeping the list to its subject. Messages which stray too much from the subject or which contain commercials are removed by the moderator. Groups function in the same way, if they are moderated the entries are examined before they are posted.

The ways of communicating may be divided according to their aspects of time. Synchronous communication takes place when the communication is done at the same time, e.g., in a chat. Asynchronous communication is when the communication takes place at different points in time, like e-mail, forums and groups.

Forums

At communities there are generally different forums. Examples of large communites (social network sites) are MySpace (www.myspace.com) and Facebook (www.facebook.com).

The concept of forum includes groups, newsgroups and similar groupings. A few examples:

- Google Groups (http://groups.google.com)
- Yahoo! Groups (http://groups.yahoo.com)

E-mail lists

Two types:

- Closed lists (one-way communication, e.g., product information)
- Open lists (everybody can send mails to the list)

Directories and lists for e-mail lists
- L-soft CataList (www.lsoft.com/catalist.html)
- Topica (http://lists.topica.com)

Interest groups and associations
Many companies, organizations and associations offer closed e-mail lists, often called newsletters.

- The Search Engine Report (http://searchenginewatch.com/sereport)
- USA Football Newsletter (www.usafootball.com/newsletter/index)

Find e-mail lists through search engines
Search on subject words together with words like:

- newsletters
- e-mail list / email list
- discussion list
- mailing list

Through searching on *mailing list library* in Google you'll find several e-mail lists with their focus on libraries.

14. Storing & Retrieving Information

During and after the information searching you will enter into another area of problems – the personal information management. How should you store that which you have found? That which is found can be everything from a link, an image or factual data to entire Web sites or reports in PDF format. There are many modes of procedure and a lot of useful services on the Web. But a central question needs to be answered first: How will the information be used?

For immediate use

Are you going to use the information directly? If you only need to read it through for background information it's often best to print it on paper. Then you can go ahead and read it with a pen in your hand. But if excerpts and perhaps images are to be used in a report you need a different kind of management. Perhaps you need to save the material as PDF files.

Save/preserve/file away

If the information needs to be saved on a more long-term basis it might be good to create PDF files of the information. The PDF files are easily created by means of a PDF writer. The contents of the PDF files can then be indexed by desktop search service to make them easily retrievable. The files can also be stored in a traditional hierarchy of folders.

For forwarding

Is it somebody else who's going to use the information? In that case it should perhaps be gathered or packaged in some way. A labour-saving way is to use a special program for this type of tasks.

For sharing with others

If several people are going to use the information a Web service may be useful. Perhaps you can store texts and links in a Web word processor or store documents in a Web hard disk.

Where should I save that which I have found?

The question which first arises is: Where should I save that which I have found? Locally on my computer or on the Web?

Locally on the computer

By saving the information on your own computer it will be quickly accessible, but only accessible on that computer. If the information is important or extensive, backup copies will have to be done, all computers can crash. Which format should the information be saved in? Only the bookmarks? PDF copies of Web pages?

On the Web

By saving the information on your own computer it's made accessible for all the connected computers, but the Web can be slow and you need to have a reliable connection. An advantage with Web storage is that you get more possibilities to share the information. At the same time you have to be on the alert when it comes to copyright, it's not allowed to make a saved Web page or image accessible on the Web without the copyright owner's permission.

How should I save that which I have found?

In a bookmark service

Many bookmark services exist on the Web today. One type consists of the so-called bookmark services where it's easy to share bookmarks and to see the number of people who also have saved the same link and who these people are. The advantage is that the bookmarks are accessible from different computers; the only thing required is to log into the services. In most of the services you can place a subject word on the links that you save; it's called to *tag* the links. By labelling the links they will be easier to find among all the bookmarks. A risk with free Web services is that the service may disappear, is taken over, is radically changed or is converted into a pay service.

- Blinklist (www.blinklist.com)
- Delicious (http://delicious.com)
- Diigo (www.diigo.com)

When you save bookmarks in the services you fill in tags (subject words) and comments. When you're logged in you can choose to see your own bookmarks or all the bookmarks in the service.

Fig. A private bookmark in Delicious.

A bookmark in Delicious is shown above. Among other things you can see that 157 persons have saved this bookmark and that it has three tags: seo, searchengine and history.

You can see and search among your own tags in a tag cloud.

Type a tag		Tags 46

Sort: Alphabetically | By size

bibliotek cloudcomputing collaboration dn docs email epost **framtiden** **google** googlegenerationen history hypertext infosök integritet **internet** **ir** konspirationsteorier kryptering **lista** map mellanhand memex ordlista osynliga productivity **säkerhet** search searchengine sem **seo** serp services software **sydsvenskan** tagging taxonomy tools **twitter** vannevarbush verktyg **web** web2.0 web20-verktyg webben wiki word,

Fig. A tag cloud in Delicious.

Delicious and other social bookmark services are described from a searcher's perspective in Chapter 3.

You find more traditional bookmark services in Google and Yahoo! (www. google.com/bookmarks/ and http://bookmarks.yahoo.com).

A list of bookmark services is found at www.feedbus.com/bookmarks/.

Services	Blinklist	Delicious	Diigo
Comment /subject word	yes/yes (lists)	yes/yes	yes/yes
Grading	yes	no	no
Local copy	no	no	yes
Private bookmarks	yes	yes	yes
Import	Internet Explorer 7 & 8, Firefox 2 & 3, Safari, Delicious	Internet Explorer 6 & 7, Firefox, Opera, Safari	Internet Explorer, Firefox, Delicious, Simpy, Blinklist, Connotea
Export	CSV, HTML, JSON	Export file for Web browser (HTML)	Internet Explorer, Netscape, RSS, CSV, Delicious
Toolbar/bookmarklets	-/yes	no/yes	yes/yes
Comment		integration in Facebook. Link roll or tag roll. RSS-feeds	can also save in other bookmark services. Publish in blog or create link roll or tag roll

Fig. Table of the function of social bookmark services.

Your own Web archive/link collection

One way of making your selected links easily available is to create your own link collection on the Net. A simple way is to put up the links you've found in a blog. But it's only the links themselves that can be saved, you can't save images or other material in this way on account of copyright (unless you password-protect the blog/Web page or make it completely private).

Sometimes you'll find scientific articles that some researcher has saved on his/her personal homepage to have within reach. The researcher has, perhaps, created a hidden link so that nobody will discover the page, but the search engine spiders are diligent and will follow all links. And with that the articles will become accessible in, e.g., Google.

On paper

The classic way is to print out Web pages and other important information. The disadvantages are that the information isn't searchable in a simple manner, and you'll need to create a physical filing system. If you're dealing with news articles or other new information a good advice would be to print it directly, as the article may be gone the next time you want to look at it. The information is often filed in the newspaper's archive which is available to subscribers and other payers.

Information on paper is easy to read and available off-line for good and worse. You don't need a computer and you can read actively with a pen in your hand.

Store links in the Web mail

The Web mail is an alternative archive. Several Web mail services offer good search possibilities (e.g., Gmail and Yahoo!) and then links and other information can be saved by mailing yourself or by mailing to a special archive mail address which is easily retrieved. This alternative is particularly useful when you're not at your own computer, but borrowing a computer temporarily.

Screen dump

A screen dump is an image of everything or parts of what is shown on the screen.

Commands:
Entire screen: shift+prtscr
Active window: alt+prtscr

Paste the screen dump into Word, PowerPoint or into an image processor. Or upload the screen dump to a blog or a Web word processor.

Gadwin PrintScreen (www.gadwin.com/printscreen/) is a freeware. The program lets you choose several file formats and zooming is possible. Another alternative is Screen grab (an addition to the Web browser Firefox).

PDF writer

Instead of printing interesting material that you find, or save entire Web sites, you can "print" the documents to a PDF writer. A PDF file is then generated which is easy to store (and to retrieve with a desktop search program). If you don't have Acrobat Writer there are free PDF writers to download.

CutePDF (www.cutepdf.com/products/cutepdf/Writer.asp) is a free PDF writer. Install the writer and print the Web pages as PDF files for future reference. Then let a desktop search service index the PDF archive. You can then search the PDF's in full text – efficient information retrieval. If you want to print out something, a PDF writer works like a test printout. On the created PDF file you'll see if everything is there and if the right parts are included in the printout. If you're dealing with long Web pages you'll even find out how many A4 pages it will be (so that you won't be surprised when the printer spits out 27 pages) and then you can print out the pages of interest to you.

"Launder" text in a text editor / collect information in txt documents

You can cut out the text and "launder" it in a text editor to save it as a text file (txt). Word-processing software like Word functions poorly, because they include too much of the text formatting, like font colour and text size.

I personally use the text editor UltraEdit both for laundering text and collecting information. In UltraEdit it's easy to work with information in different subjects as this text editor works with tabs. Thanks to the tabs it's easy to have many documents open and to shift between them.

Notebooks and word processors on the Net

Word processors and notebooks on the Net are other good ways for saving information, particularly if you need to be able to reach it from different computers. Google Docs is one example of a Web-based word processor and it allows several people to collaborate on the documents. Other features are connections to online publishing and blogging.

Save searches

Save the URL to the search engine's hit list among your favourites so that you easily can go back and do the exact same search later.

Special programs

There is a type of programs called *research managers*. In these programs you can save Web pages, text excerpts, images and other things from the Web for later use of the material, for the creation of reports or for the use of the information in other programs. The saved material can be labelled with comments, subject words and other meta data. In some programs you can, supposedly, also save copies of entire Web sites. Several of the large programs have gone from being just programs to being Web services. eSnips (www.esnips.com) is one Web-based service.

Tools like eSnips will probably be getting increasingly more significance in the future when the utilization of the Web generally, and of information management tools specifically, will come to maturity. We will no longer be able to afford or have the time to find information which we will later lose again. The utilization will have to be rendered more efficient. What does it matter that everybody has broadband if nobody can save a text snippet in a sensible way?

Desktop search programs

To find your way among downloaded or created files you may have great use of a desktop search program. The program works like a local search engine; it creates an index of the content in your hard disk or in certain directories. Make sure that the program actually indexes the file types that are important to you. Also check if the program indexes other units than your ordinary hard disk (C:). This is especially important if you are connected to a network where you use files from different network units.

At the time of writing the largest desktop search programs are the following:

- Copernic Desktop Search (www.copernic.com/en/products/desktop-search/
- Windows Desktop Search (www.microsoft.com/windows/products/winfamily/desktopsearch/default.mspx)
- Yahoo! Desktop Search (http://us.config.toolbar.yahoo.com/yds)

- Google Desktop Search (http://desktop.google.com)
- Exalead (www.exalead.com/software/products/desktop-search/)

Case study – desktop search

For a long time I had been looking for an old version of my thesis manuscript on my hard disk. But since the documents on the computer had turned into a muddle of folders and files from several old computers (private-, study- and work computers) I couldn't find the file. I was after the title of my submitted thesis manuscript, but I didn't know what the file name could be. But then suddenly one day it hit me: I had added the ISSN of the publication series on the title page! I could then search on that number in my desktop search program (Copernic Desktop Search) because it had indexed all the files on the computer. No sooner said than done. At the search the document showed up among the oldest ones in the hit list (and with an insignificant name). I had retrieved the sought title!

Index the content in Thunderbird

Are you using Mozilla Thunderbird for your RSS feeds? You can then index the posts by means of, for example, Copernic Desktop Search. Priceless if you normally spend time looking for posts where you've read something important. Naturally the e-mail in both Thunderbird and Outlook can be indexed.

15. Monitoring – Passive Searching

It's easy to be updated in a simple way!

Active and passive searching

Information searching can take a lot of time, too much time. But there are ways to do passive searches, so that the information will come to you. The incoming information must, however, be sifted; only a small part are grains of gold.

According to Marcia Bates (Professor in Information Science) the most common way of searching for information is passive searching. Passive searching means that you make use of the information when it shows up, you don't search for it actively. The passive searching takes much less time and energy than the active one.[1]

The best is to combine the two methods. You actively create structures which can deliver the information, structures that you then passively check up on.

Standing search in search engine

Through so-called alerts you'll receive a mail when new hits enter the hit list (normally the top 50 or 100) for a specific search. Google's own alert service (beta) (www.google.com/alerts):

---

1 Bates, M.J. (2002). Toward An Integrated Model of Information Seeking and Searching. http://www.gseis.ucla.edu/faculty/bates/articles/info_SeekSearch-i-030329.html

Fig. Google's alert mail for the "invisible web" OR "deep web". The mail is divided into three parts: News Alert, Blogs Alert and Web Alert.

Before searches done in Live could be delivered via RSS, but at the time of writing Bing lacks that function. Further on in this chapter you'll find more information about RSS.

Web site monitoring

Both Web-based services and locally installed software monitor Web pages. They make a copy of the page which they are set to monitor. They then return, in accordance with the settings, and make a new copy which will be compared to the old one. If anything has been changed, added or in come cases removed on the page, a message will be sent, a so-called alert.

One problem is that simple changes on a Web page, like a changed date, results in an "alert". In some services you can, when the monitoring begins, determine that, e.g., at least five words need be changed in order for a change to be reported.

When is it good to use a Web page monitor?

- ♦ When the information isn't accessible via RSS (see further on in the chapter for more information about RSS).

- For Web sites without RSS. Many information-rich Web sites lack RSS. Or only selected parts are published with RSS, e.g., press releases.
- When you're looking for specific information. Perhaps it's only a subpage with a special topic or service that is to be monitored, e.g, the personnel page of an organization to see if there have been any new hirings or if there are any vacancies.
- To keep track of news or updatings by monitoring, e.g., the first page or the news page of a Web site, a Web guide's page for "new updates" or the "news page" of an organization. In this way you'll get indications of changes and of things that are in the works, without having to monitor a large quantity of pages.

Most Web pages will change at some point. To visit all the interesting pages regularly takes a lot of time and is inefficient. Examples of use are to keep a check on a company page with vacancies or a company's Web page for new books.

Different delivery ways:

- e-mail
- RSS
- within the service or program

Register the Web address and choose settings: How often should the page be checked and how should the message be delivered? Also check to make sure that the mail from the service won't get caught in a spam filter.

Different services have different possibilities. They may use alerts at:

- change of a certain size (kb)
- if certain words or phrases are used
- if certain words don't occur
- change in link, image or date
- certain number of changes (number of words or signs).

Differences in that which is reported:

- changes
- new content
- removed content.

Problems:

- Web addresses that change (the old one is monitored but not the new one)
- Free alert services may disappear (note which pages are monitored by which service)
- Problems with monitoring search engine- unfriendly pages with frames, scripts etc.

Free services	Changedetect	www.changedetect.com
	Feedwhip	www.feedwhip.com
	Follow that page	www.followthatpage.com
	Trackengine	www.trackengine.com
	Trackle	www.trackle.com
	Urlwatch	www.urlwatch.org
	Watchthat-page	www.watchthatpage.com
	Webagent	www.webagent.nl
Pay services	Infominder	www.infominder.com/webminder
	Tracerlock	www.tracerlock.com
Software	Website-watcher	www.aignes.com
	Copernic tracker	www.copernic.com/en/products/tracker

Fig. Different monitoring services and programs

Software

Web-site monitor programs let you keep track of lots of Web pages, without you having to be out on the Web yourself. A couple of examples (which you can download and test for free):

WebSite-Watcher is a program that checks whether the monitored Web pages have been changed. You don't have to surf in and check it. (www.aignes.com)

Copernic (which has a good *desktop search program*) has a Web-site monitor program, Copernic Tracker, in the same style as WebSite-Watcher. (www.copernic.com/en/products/tracker)

Web services

WatchThatPage (www.watchthatpage.com) is a Web service which monitors Web pages for you. When pages are changed a mail with the changes is sent. Watch-ThatPage sends the changes on the page as text, but you can't see where on the page the changes have been made. TrackEngine (www.trackengine.com), however, shows the entire page with the changes marked out.

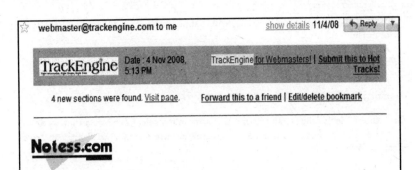

Notess.com

"On the Net" in *Online*

A column covering information resources and capabilities on the Internet
by Greg R. Notess

Published in *Online* since 1993, this column features information resources and tools available on the
Internet and the World Wide Web, specifically ones of interest to information professionals. Originally
entitled "On the Nets" and covering BITNET, Usenet, and the Internet, we dropped the plural and made
it "On the Net" starting with the July 1997 issue. The following list includes columns and the
occasional article in *Online*. Most are linked to full-text online versions. See also my related columns:
On the Net in *Database* 1993-1999 and **Web Wanderings** in *EContent* Feb.-Dec. 2000.

ONLINE

- "Finding Free Media." 33(1): forthcoming, Jan.-Feb. 2009.
- "The Downside of Upgrades." 32(6): 42-44, Nov.-Dec. 2008.
- "A Potpourri of 2.0 Tools." 32(5):43-45, Sept.-Oct. 2008.
- "Searching the Twitter Realm." 32(4): 43-45, July-Aug. 2008.
- Multilingual Searching: Search Engine Language Tools. 32(3): 40-42, May-June. 2008.
- Speed Searching 32(2): 41-44, Mar.-Apr. 2008.
- An About Face on Facebook? 32(1): 43-45, Jan.-Feb. 2008.
- The Incredible, Embedded Web. 31(5): 43-46, Sept.-Oct. 2007.

*Fig. Alert message via e-mail from TrackEngine. The highlighted (grey) four
lines with bullets are the four new sections on the monitored Web page.*

E-mail alerts

Alerts via mail is a service provided by some Web sites. You'll get mails when
pages have been updated or when new documents have been published that match
the criteria you have set up.

An advantage here is that mail alerts give fewer "false positive results" than RSS
flows and Web site monitors. The mails are only sent when something is added,
and then you have to set up good criteria for the service, to choose the right subject
or formulate a good search query. In some services you'll be notified of all changes

within a certain part of the Web site, and that of course leads to less precision and more noise.

You can find different specific alert services via e-mail by searching on: *"e-mail alerts" OR "email alerts"* together with subject words like, e.g.:

"e-mail alerts" OR "email alerts" "oil price"

On Yahoo! Alerts (alerts.yahoo.com) there are many selectable alerts such as news or events at the Yahoo! auctions. Unfortunately there is no possibilitiy to have alerts on Web searches.

Google Alerts (www.google.com/alerts) is, however, a service entirely concentrated on Web searches, blogs and news. Googlealert (www.googlealert.com) is an alert service completely independent from Google but that searches in Google.

RSS

What is RSS?

RSS is a simple XML format for distribution of, among other things, news headlines on the Web. Whole or parts of Web-based text paragraphs are sent together with a link to the original material. You can read the RSS flow in an RSS reader (also called a news aggregator), and in more recent Web browsers the function is built in. A format which works as RSS is Atom, but it's not an RSS standard. RSS consists of several standards:

♦   RDF Site Summary (RSS 0.9 and 1.0)
♦   Rich Site Summary (RSS 0.9x)
♦   Really Simple Syndication (RSS 2.x)

It doesn't matter which type of RSS flow you're dealing with, or if it's Atom, as long as the RSS reader can manage it. RSS flows are often marked with an orange icon:

Fig. RSS symbol used by the major Web readers.

Make use of RSS

RSS can be used for many things:

Alerts via RSS

Via Live Search you can have standing searches where you get the results via RSS instead of e-mail. In databases there are also RSS alerts for standing searches, e.g., the medical database PubMed (www.ncbi.nlm.nih.gov/sites/entrez).

News with RSS

Many news suppliers have RSS feeds. By subscribing to RSS you can easily keep up with the headlines without having to visit the Web sites and you can easily monitor everything from local to international news.

Follow blogs with RSS

Subscribe to RSS feeds and read the blog entries in one spell or when they pop up in your RSS reader. You don't have to go to the Web sites and actually be on the lookout; particularly good if the blog is published irregularly.

- Follow blogs without visiting them.
- Take home posts and file them away for future needs.
- Save the posts without any sifting.
- Index the posts with a desktop search service.
- Search your own archive when need arises.

Monitor Web sites with RSS

Web sites often have RSS feeds for news of different types, e.g., press releases, technical news or product information.

RSS readers

The RSS readers can be divided into four groups:

- Completely Web-based readers that don't require any installation on your computer and that can be reached from anywhere on the Net (e.g., Bloglines, www.bloglines.com).
- Desktop readers which are programs on your computer (require installation) and that can only be used at one specific computer (e.g., Mozilla Thunderbird).
- Hybrid readers which are readers that work as Web-based readers but with programs to install to increase the functionality.
- Integrated readers which are functions in another program, e.g., a Web browser.

Mozilla Thunderbird (www.mozilla.org) is an RSS reader (and an e-mail program). In Thunderbird it's easy to set up subscriptions to RSS feeds. The feeds are separate and you'll have to check the different sources separately. Nothing is discarded automatically in Thunderbird; in some Web services there may be an upper time limit that regulates how long the entries will be saved.

How you find feeds (1)

The easiest way to find feeds is to go to the Web site that interests you and look for links that contain RSS or XML. There are often links to the RSS feeds at the very bottom of the foot of the page. Sometimes the easiest way is to search on RSS in the search function of the Web site.

You then put these links (URL's) into the RSS reader. The easiest way is to copy and paste the links. In some cases you can also have them put in automatically into your reader (see below).

Sometimes there are various simple ways of adding the flow to your favourite reader. There are links or buttons to: Feedburner, Rojo, MyMSN, Bloglines, myFeedster, NewsGator, Pluck, My Yahoo! and Google. This is often the case on pages with an IT focus; there are lots of shortcuts for the insertion into different readers.

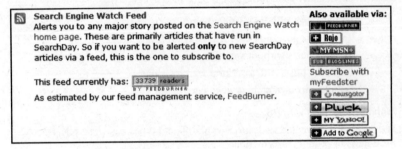

Fig. RSS fast links at searchenginewatch.com.

How you find feeds (2)

Another way to find feeds is to use search services for RSS feeds. Some of the services are:

- Feedster (http://feedster.com)
- Syndic8 (www.syndic8.com)
- RSS Network (www.rss-network.com)

How you find feeds (3)

Both Internet Explorer 7 and Mozilla Firefox 2 have an automatic function to discover RSS feeds. In Internet Explorer the RSS symbol, located to the right of the tabs, is lighted.

Fig. The RSS symbol lighted in Internet Explorer.

In Internet Explorer you can choose among the Web site's different RSS feeds by clicking on the little arrow next to the symbol. When you come to the page of the chosen RSS feed you can click on the star with the plus sign to the left of the tab (see the image above). After that you choose where to place the folder of the feed.

In Firefox the RSS symbol is shown in the address box. By clicking on it you can choose which of the RSS feed at Wikipedia.org you want to subscribe to.

Fig. The RSS symbol in Mozilla Firefox.

When you have chosen an RSS feed you will choose where in the Web browser it should be placed, among the bookmarks or in the bookmark box. Each RSS feed creates a new folder in which the posts are collected.

Then the selected RSS feed automatically update the contents of the folder where the latest posts are always shown.

16. Useful Programs

For efficient information searching on the Net some software is required. Certain programs are necessary, whereas others will provide increased functionality or more possibilities.

Web browsers

A recent version of a Web browser will have many features that the older versions lack. In both Internet Explorer 7.0 (or later) and Mozilla Firefox there is the possibilitiy of working with *tabs*. Tabs mean that you can have several Web pages open in the same Web browser, though in different tabs. The illustrations below show two tabs each in Internet Explorer and Firefox, Washington Post and Los Angels Times.

Fig. Tabs in Internet Explorer 8.0.

Fig. Tabs in Mozilla Firefox 3.5.

By clicking on the tab to a Web page this page will be on top in the Web browser. If you find an interesting link on a Web page but want to finish reading the Web page first, without forgetting about the link, you can choose "open in a new tab" and the link will be opened in a new tab in the Web browser. If you have forgotten that you've opened the tab you will, in most cases, discover it when you clear the tabs.

Other web browsers are:

+ Google Chrome (www.google.com/chrome)
+ Opera (www.opera.com)
+ Safari (www.apple.com/safari/)

Portable Web browser

The Web browser Mozilla Firefox exists in a portable variant, Portable Firefox. Portable Firefox is an adaptation of the ordinary Firefox so that you can run it from, e.g., a USB memory stick or a portable hard disk. By running the Web browser from, e.g., a USB memory stick you can take with you settings, bookmarks and extra functions that you have installed. The Web browser will be a bit slower to start up and also a bit slower to use. Another problem is that many computers in public environments are limited as to their possibility to run programs from movable units. (http://portableapps.com/apps/internet/firefox_portable)

Toolbars

Practically all commercial search services now offer downloadable toolbars for installation in the Web browser.

Fig. Google's toolbar is shown in the lower part of the image.

The toolbars facilitate searches in a particular service; the search will be faster as it won't be necessary to download the homepage of the service. The search services thus also create more loyal users (customers really, as they make their living from the display of advertising) in that the user becomes somewhat more tied to the service as it will be more tiresome to search in another service. All toolbars have different extra functions, e.g., the blocking of pop-up windows. At the same time there are lots of toolbars that really should be considered to be spy programs. The first warning sign is the name of the toolbar. If it's called Google or Yahoo! it's probably okay, but if you don't know about the company or the service you have reason to be suspicious. Another warning sign is if you have installed the toolbar consciously or if it has "installed itself". Unless you've done an active choice there's probably something fishy about it. A third sign of warning is if the toolbar is difficult to uninstall, in this case you would not be dealing with a serious company.

Programs for problem-free searching

One Web browser is often not enough to be successful with your information searching. It's generally required that the computer be able to show different kinds of files, like PDF or DOC. Perhaps different types of media players are needed to be able to play the sound- or video files that you've found. Today many modern Web sites also require new versions of, e.g., Java and Flash to function in the way the designer has imagined.

Office programs
* MS Office (http://office.microsoft.com)
* MS Office Reader (www.microsoft.com/downloads/)
* Open Office (www.openoffice.org)
* Lotus Symphony (http://symphony.lotus.com)

PDF readers

Acrobat Reader or other PDF reader. You find Acrobat Reader at www.adobe.com

Media players

* Windows Media Player (www.microsoft.com/downloads/)
* QuickTime (www.apple.com/quicktime/download/)
* Real Player (www.real.com)

Other programs

* Java (www.java.com)
* Flash (http://get.adobe.com/flashplayer/)
* Shockwave (http://get.adobe.com/shockwave/)

Download programs

* http://download.cnet.com
* www.tucows.com

Check the links in Favourites

AM-DeadLink is a freeware program which checks in Favourites for dead links, links that don't work any longer. Works with Internet Explorer, Opera and Mozilla Firefox. (http://aignes.net/ deadlink.htm)

Compressed files

* www.filzip.com
* http://7-zip.org

Web-based programs

All kinds of programs can now be found in Web-based versions. It's called cloud-computing and the type of services are called Software as a Service (SaaS).

Calendar	Google Calendar	www.google.com/calendar
To remember	Remember the milk	www.rememberthemilk.com
Notes	Google Notebook	www.google.com/notebook/
Office programs	Google Docs and spreadsheets	http://docs.google.com
	Zoho Office Suite	http://zoho.com
	ThinkFree	www.thinkfree.com
	Ajax13	http://us.ajax13.com/en/
	Office Live Workspace	www.officelive.com
Projects	Basecamp	http://basecamphq.com

	Central Desktop	www.centraldesktop.com
Spell-check	Orangoo Spell Check	http://orangoo.com/spell/
Image processing	myImager.com	http://myimager.com
	Pixlr	www.pixlr.com
	Photoshop.com	www.photoshop.com
File conversion	Zamzar (beta)	http://zamzar.com
Storage	Box	http://box.net
	Adrive	www.adrive.com

Web desktop – Desktop on the Net

Instead of departing from your own computer's desktop (operating system and programs) there are similar services on the Net where the programs or the functions and storage possibilities are completely on-line. These Web-based services create an independence from a certain computer where your documents are saved, but at the same time the condition for these services is that the ones offering the Web services keep the services active and working. Netvibes.com is a desktop service to which you can connect other Web services, e.g., the content in the Net hard disk Box.net and the mail in Gmail.com and also the RSS flows that interest you.

+ www.netvibes.com
+ www.pageflakes.com
+ www.protopage.com
+ www.google.com/ig

File types

General file types are presented here. The common ones come first followed by image, sound and media and at the end streaming media.

TXT (Text)

Format for pure text. Doesn't save any formatting, only ASCII-based signs.

Can be opened in, e.g., Notes or Wordpad in Windows (and in all word processing programs).

HTML (Hypertext Markup Language)

A page description language for documents on the Web. Read in a Web browser, e.g., Internet Explorer or Mozilla Firefox.

PDF (Portable Document Format)

PDF files are fixed (rastered) and will keep the formatting irrespective of computer system. Consequently the format has become standard for documents that are transferred between computers. Printed material that also is published on the Web is often in PDF format exactly because it was originally produced for printing.

Acrobat Reader is a free reader available at: www.adobe.com/products/acrobat/readstep2.html

To create PDF files the program Adobe Acrobat or some other PDF program is required. A PDF writer, a program which works as a writer, also works well, e.g., CutePDF Writer, (www.cutepdf.com/Products/CutePDF/writer.asp).

PS (PostScript)

PostScript is a page description language (like HTML) which is used for print-outs. The more expensive printers are often PS printers and the file which the computer sends to the printer is in PS. PS files were sometimes put out on the Internet before the launching of PDF. (To simplify matters you could say that PDF is a light variant of PS).

DOC (Word Document)

The format which is used by the word processor Microsoft Word. The format is getting increasingly complex and files created in a new version of Word can't always be opened in an older version. Can be opened in OpenOffice (www.openoffice.org). There are also free readers to download from Microsoft - Word Viewer 2003 (search in Google). DOCX is the new file type used in Word 2007 (Office 2007). It can be opened in older versions of Word if you download the "Microsoft Office Compatibility Pack" from Microsoft.com.

XLS (Excel Worksheet)

The format used by the spreadsheet program Microsoft Excel. Can be opened in OpenOffice (www.openoffice.org). There are also free readers to download from Microsoft - Excel Viewer 2003 (search in Google).

PPT (PowerPoint Presentation)

The format used by the presentation program Microsoft PowerPoint. Can be opened in OpenOffice (www.openoffice.org). There are also free readers to download from Microsoft - PowerPoint Viewer 2003 (search in Google).

Image

You won't normally have any problems opening the common image formats in Windows or mounting these in an office program (e.g., Word or Power Point). Image formats which may be hard to mount are EPS and images saved as PDF.

To convert images into a format there are lots of programs, e.g., Batch Converter. In Batch Converter you can convert many images at once. A test version of the program is free for evaluation (www.batchconverter.com/image-converter.html).

In ordinary graphic programs you also have the possibility through "save as" or "export" to choose another file format for the images than the original one.

JPEG / JPG (Joint Photographic Experts Group)
Image format for colour images that removes certain data to make the files smaller.

TIFF / TIF (Tagged Image File Format)
TIFF images can be in just any resolution, and they can be in black and white, in a grey scale or in colour.

GIF (Graphics Interchange Format)
Image format used on the Web. The format is limited to 256 colours and is therefore principally used for scanned images (illustrations, not photos).

BMP (Bitmap Graphics)
The standard format for images (pixel) in Windows.

PNG (Portable Network Graphics)
A new image format intended to replace the GIF on the Web as the PNG doesn't contain any patented algorithms (completely free from patents and licences).

EPS (Encapsulated PostScript)
EPS is the image format in PostScript. There are two types of EPS files:

(1) A vector-based image format (not pixels) that can be opened in Adobe Illustrator and similar programs. These files can be mounted/imported to Word, Pagemaker etc. but can't be opened by the programs. You can change the scale of these images (object graphics) as much as you want without altering the images.

(2) An EPS photo file (pixels) and with a fixed resolution. The file type can be opened in Photoshop or similar programs and it can be mounted/imported to Word, Pagemaker etc. You can only change the scale of the images in the same way as you can with other pixel-based image formats.

Sound

MP3 (MPEG, Audio Layer 3)
Sound format. As the files are rather small they are easy to transfer via the Internet. Or use in an MP3 player.

WMA (Windows Media Audio File)
A Microsoft format for compressed digital sound files, resembles MP3.

WAV (Waveform Audio)

A format for raw sound files, often used as a source for other formats (that are compressed). The format is developed by IBM and Microsoft together and can be played by almost all Windows programs that support sound.

Media

MPEG-1

MPEG stands for Motion Pictures Expert Group, an expert group put together to develop the digital formats that we have today. One part of the MPEG-1 is the sound format MP3.

MP4 (MPEG-4 Video File)

MP4 9 is a more advanced media file type than MPEG-1.

AVI (Audio Video Interleave File)

A format which is developed by Microsoft for the storing of sound and video. The files are limited to a resolution of 320 x 240 and 30 images per second (not enough for full-screen video). You can record videos with many digital cameras and that is then in the AVI format.

Streaming media

Streaming media is sound (like radio) or video (like TV) which is downloaded at the same time as it's played back. The files in themselves are not saved (special programs are required to do this, see below).

In streaming media there are three big actors:

- Real Networks (RealMedia, RealVideo and RealAudio)
- Microsoft (Windows Media - audio and video)
- Apple (QuickTime)

You find links to media players below. If you just have one (or one of each) modern media player installed you won't normally have any problem with listening to/seeing "the broadcasting".

Record (save down) streaming media – lots of links to programs at http://all-streaming-media.com.

Media players

To play the media files a player is required. Windows often includes Windows Media Player. If this doesn't work, you might need to download a newer version or another player.

Common media players are (they regularly come in new versions):

- Windows Media Player (www.microsoft.com/windows/windowsmedia/default.mspx)
- QuickTime Player (www.apple.com/quicktime/download/win.html)
- Real Player (www.real.com/realplayer)

Resources

FILExt - The File Extension Source (http://filext.com)

Webopedia (www.webopedia.com)

ComputerUser - dictionary (www.computeruser.com/resources/dictionary/)

Streaming media FAQ (http://all-streaming-media.com/streaming-media-faq/)

Appendix A.
Top Domains

National

AC Ascension Island
AD Andorra
AE United Arab Emirates
AF Afghanistan
AG Antigua and Barbuda
AI Anguilla
AL Albania
AM Armenia
AN Netherlands Antilles
AO Angola
AQ The Antarctis
AR Argentina
AS American Samoa
AT Austria
AU Australia
AW Aruba
AZ Azerbaijan

BA Bosnia/Hercegovina
BB Barbados
BD Bangladesh
BE Belgium
BF Burkina Faso
BG Bulgaria
BH Bahrain
BI Burundi
BJ Benin
BM Bermuda
BN Brunei
BO Bolivia
BR Brasil
BS Bahamas
BT Bhutan
BV Bouvet Island

BW Botswana
BY Belarus
BZ Belize

CA Canada
CC Cocos (Keeling) Islands
CD Congo, Democratic Republic of the
CF Central African Republic
CG Congo, Republic of the
CH Switzerland
CI Cote D'Ivoire
CK Cook Islands
CL Chile
CM Cameroon
CN China
CO Colombia
CR Costa Rica
CU Cuba
CV Cap Verde
CX Christmas Island
CY Cyprus
CZ Czech Republic

DE Germany
DJ Djibouti
DK Denmark
DM Dominica
DO Dominican Republic
DZ Algeria

EC Ecuador
EE Estonia
EG Egypt
EH Western Sahara

ER Eritrea
ES Spain
ET Ethiopia

FI Finland
FJ Fiji
FK Falkland Islands (Islas Malvinas)
FM Micronesia, Federated States of
FO Faroe Islands
FR France

GA Gabon
GD Grenada
GE Georgia
GF French Guiana
GG Guernsey
GH Ghana
GI Gibraltar
GL Greenland
GM Gambia, The
GN Guinea
GP Guadeloupe
GQ Equatorial Guinea
GR Greece
GS South Georgia and the South Sand-
wich Islands
GT Guatemala
GU Guam
GW Guinea-Bissau
GY Guyana

HK Hong Kong
HM Heard Island and McDonald Is-
lands
HN Honduras
HR Croatia (Hrvatska)
HT Haiti
HU Hungary

ID Indonesia
IE Ireland
IL Israel
IM Isle of Man
IN India
IO British Indian Ocean Territory
IQ Iraq

IR Iran
IS Iceland
IT Italy

JE Jersey
JM Jamaica
JO Jordan
JP Japan

KE Kenya
KG Kyrgyzstan
KH Cambodia
KI Kiribati
KM Comoros
KN Saint Kitts and Nevis
KP North Korea
KR South Korea
KW Kuwait
KY Cayman Islands
KZ Kazakhstan

LA Laos
LB Lebanon
LC Saint Lucia
LI Lichtenstein
LK Sri Lanka
LR Liberia
LS Lesotho
LT Lithuania
LU Luxembourg
LV Latvia
LY Libya

MA Morocco
MC Monaco
MD Moldova
MG Madagascar
MH Marshall Islands
MK Macedonia
ML Mali
MM Myanmar (Burma)
MN Mongolia
MO Macau
MP Northern Mariana Islands
MQ Martinique
MR Mauritania

MS Montserrat
MT Malta
MU Mauritius
MV Maldives
MW Malawi
MX Mexico
MY Malaysia
MZ Mozambique

NA Namibia
NC New Caledonia
NE Niger
NF Norfolk Islands
NG Nigeria
NI Nicaragua
NL Netherlands
NO Norway
NP Nepal
NR Nauru
NU Niue
NZ New Zealand

OM Oman

PA Panama
PE Peru
PF French Polynesia
PG Papua New Guinea
PH Philippines
PK Pakistan
PL Poland
PM St. Pierre and Miquelon
PN Pitcairn Islands
PR Puerto Rico
PS Palestine
PT Portugal
PW Palau
PY Paraguay

QA Qatar

RE Reunion Island
RO Romania
RU Russia
RW Rwanda

SA Saudi Arabia
SB Solomon Islands
SC Seychelles
SD Sudan
SE Sweden
SG Singapore
SH St. Helena
SI Slovenia
SJ Svalbard and Jan Mayen Islands
SK Slovakia
SL Sierra Leone
SM San Marino
SN Senegal
SO Somalia
SR Suriname
ST Sao Tome and Principe
SV El Salvador
SY Syria
SZ Swaziland

TC Turks and Caicos Islands
TD Chad
TF French Southern Territories
TG Togo
TH Thailand
TJ Tajikistan
TK Tokelau
TM Turkmenistan
TN Tunisia
TO Tonga
TP East Timor
TR Turkey
TT Trinidad and Tobago
TV Tuvalu
TW Taiwan
TZ Tanzania

UA Ukraine
UG Uganda
UK United Kingdom
UM US Minor Outlying Islands
US United States
UY Uruguay
UZ Uzbekistan

VA Holy See (Vatican City)

VC St Vincent and the Grenadines
VE Venezuela
VG Virgin Islands (British)
VI Virgin Islands (USA)
VN Vietnam
VU Vanuatu

WF Wallis and Futuna Islands
WS Samoa

YE Yemen
YT Mayotte
YU Yugoslavia

ZA South Africa
ZM Zambia
ZW Zimbabwe

General
AERO air-transport industry
ARPA ARPAnet

BIZ businesses

COM commercial
COOP cooperatives

EDU educational institution
EU European Union

FED federal (US Government)

GOV goverment (US Government)

INFO information
INT international organizations

MIL military (US department of defence)
MOBI pages adapted to mobile devices
MUSEUM museums

NAME individuals
NATO Nato
NET net operators

ORG organizations

PRO professional

TRAVEL travel-related businesses

Appendix B. Further Reading

Books

Battelle, John (2005). *The search: how Google and its rivals rewrote the rules of business and transformed our culture.* New York: Portfolio

Bell, Suzanne S. (2006). *Librarian's guide to online searching.* Westport, Conn.: Libraries Unlimited

Calishain, Tara. (2007). *Information trapping: real-time research on the web.* Berkeley, Calif.: New Riders

Calishain, Tara (2005). *Web search garage.* Upper Saddle River, N.J.: Prentice Hall PTR

Clyde, Laurel A. (2004). *Weblogs and libraries.* Oxford: Chandos

Fielden, Ned L. & Kuntz, Lucy (2002). *Search engines handbook.* Jefferson, NC: McFarland & Co

Friedman, Barbara G. (2004). *Web search savvy: strategies and shortcuts for online research.* Mahwah, N.J.: Lawrence Erlbaum

Hartmann, Karen & Ackermann, Ernest (2004). *Searching and Researching on the Internet and the World Wide Web.*

Hock, Randolph & Notess, Greg R. (2007). *The extreme searcher's Internet handbook: a guide for the serious searcher.* 2. ed. Medford, N.J.: CyberAge Books

Levene, Mark (2006). *An introduction to search engines and Web navigation.* Harlow: Addison-Wesley

Marchionini, Gary (1995). *Information seeking in electronic environments.* Cambridge: Cambridge Univ. Press

Miller, Michael (2009). *Googlepedia: the ultimate Google resource.* 3rd ed. Indianapolis, Ind.: Que

Notess, Greg R. (2006). *Teaching web search skills: techniques and strategies of top trainers.* Medford, N.J.: Information Today

Pedley, Paul (2001). *The invisible web: searching the hidden parts of the internet.* London: Aslib IMI

Schlein, Alan M. (2004). *Find It Online: The Complete Guide to Online Research.* Tempe, Ariz.: Facts on demand

Sherman, Chris. (2005). *Google power: unleash the full potential of Google.* Berkeley, Calif.: Osborne/McGraw-Hill

Sherman, Chris (2001). *The invisible web: uncovering information sources search engines can't see.* Medford, N.J.: Information Today

Stacey, Alison & Stacey, Adrian (2004). *Effective information retrieval from the Internet: an advanced user's guide.* Oxford: Chandos

Vise, David A. & Malseed, Mark (2006). *The Google story.* New ed. London: Pan Macmillan

Witten, Ian H., Gori, Marco & Numerico, Teresa (2006). *Web dragons: inside the myths of search engine technology.* Boston: Morgan Kaufmann

Reports

Bergman, Michael K. (2001). "The 'Deep' Web: Surfacing Hidden Value." Deep Web White Paper. http://www.brightplanet.com/component/content/article/23-details/119-the-deep-web-surfacing-hidden-value.html

Bergman, Michael K. (2004). "Guide to Effective Searching of the Internet – 2005." http://www.brightplanet.com/component/content/article/23-details/112-guide-to-effective-searching-of-the-internet.html

Web resources

Finding Information on the Internet: A Tutorial (UC Berkeley Library)
http://www.lib.berkeley.edu/TeachingLib/Guides/Internet/FindInfo.html

Internet Tutorials (University Libraries, SUNY Albany)
http://internettutorials.net

Pandia Search Central (also newsletters)
http://www.pandia.com

ResearchBuzz (also newsletters)
http://www.researchbuzz.com

Search Engine Land (also newsletters)
http://searchengineland.com/

Search Engine Watch (also newsletters)
http://searchenginewatch.com

Index

e-mail lists 127, 128
Exalead 135

F

facet searching 65
facts services 121
field searching 78, 119
file types 150
  images 151
  media 153
  sound 152
  text 150
find RSS feeds 144
forums 127
fresh Web 104

G

general directories 29, 30
general top domains 158
Google 17, 20, 22, 25
  PageRank 22
  quick guide 81
  ranking 23
Google Chrome 147
Google Desktop Search 135
graphic hit lists 43
groups 127

H

hidden Web 97
hit list
  graphic 43
  horizontal 42
  vertical 42
horizontal hit list 42
HTML 10
HTTP 9

I

indexer 18
Infomine 33
information need 57
information seeking 63
Internet 9

Internet Explorer 147
inverse document frequency 21
inverted index 20
invisible Web 97, 107
  contains 99
  different types of 100
  really invisible Web 104
  reasons for invisibility 99
  searching the invisible Web 108
  search strategies 109
  what is 98
IP number 10

K

Kartoo 44

L

LCSH 32
Librarians' Internet Index 30, 32, 33
link analysis 22
link collections 29, 34
link farms 95
link popularity 22
links as commodities 91

M

manipulation of search engines 94
media knowledge 88
media players 149, 153
Metacrawler 40
meta search services 39
  commercial links 40
  hit list 40
  orgin of the links 39
  search in 41
meta tags 13
misspelt Web addresses 95
monitoring 137
Mozilla Firefox 147
Mozilla Thunderbird 135

N

national top domains 155
non-existent Web 105